TRANSFORM YOUR CHURCH
WITH MINISTRY TEAMS

Transform Your Church with Ministry Teams

E. Stanley Ott

WILLIAM B. EERDMANS PUBLISHING COMPANY
GRAND RAPIDS, MICHIGAN / CAMBRIDGE, U.K.

Wm. B. Eerdmans Publishing Co.
255 Jefferson Ave. S.E., Grand Rapids, Michigan 49503 /
P.O. Box 163, Cambridge CB3 9PU U.K.
www.eerdmans.com

Printed in the United States of America

09 08 07 06 05 04   7 6 5 4 3 2 1

Library of Congress Cataloging-in-Publication Data

Ott, E. Stanley, 1948-
Transform your church with ministry teams / E. Stanley Ott.
p.   cm.
Includes bibliographical references.
ISBN 0-8028-2233-9 (pbk.: paper)
1. Church renewal. 2. Group ministry. I. Title.
BV600.3.O75 2004

253'.7 — dc22

2004047167

To Tom Saxon
— friend of the heart —
and superb ministry-team leader

CONTENTS

Appendixes

Transformational congregations are springing up everywhere. Just as the word "conform" means to change the shape of something, so the word "transform" means to change the very nature of something. "And do not be *conformed* to this world, but be *transformed* by the renewing of your minds . . ." (Romans 12:2a, NRSV, my emphasis). Transformation means change — changed lives and changed ways of experiencing congregational life.

Ministry teams are one of the fastest-growing shifts in approach to congregational leadership today, and they are essential to the transformational congregation. Imagine the passion and excitement of the twelve apostles at the idea of being with and serving Jesus Christ when he called them, "that they might be with him and that he might send them out to preach" (Mark 3:14). Imagine the responsibility the two disciples felt when Jesus sent them to prepare the Upper Room for the Passover, or the excitement his disciples felt when he sent seventy of them, two by two, to heal the sick and to bear witness to the Kingdom of God. These biblical examples demonstrate the point I want to make here: There is no greater sense of passion than the one that grows when you undertake a mission on behalf of Jesus Christ and do it with others who are also loved and sent by Christ.

Ministry teams are just such missional and ministry-minded groups. They multiply in the life of transformational congregations and have a major impact on the lives of the people in those congregations and in their surrounding communities. They foster friendships among their members and "grow" them into disciples, and together they pursue a common vision with incredible passion.

In contrast to the deployment of transformational ministry teams, traditional church leadership uses a committee structure to accomplish its work. When well done, this approach can be a very effective one. However, committees are almost always task-driven, and only rarely do they facilitate personal friendships among their members and intentionally develop their discipleship as well as accomplish their mission. Ministry teams perform all three functions.

Ministry teams predispose members to move forward with passion and enthusiasm, whereas committees are inclined to safeguard present activities and move slowly. Ministry teams get energized with new ideas, whereas committees worry about setting a precedent. Ministry teams are learning organizations, whereas committees are continuing organizations. Of course, you may have been part of a committee that did its work with passion, vigor, and impact, but I think you see the general point I'm making. Committees tend toward maintenance, while teams tend toward movement. A ministry team develops its members and acts with considerably more passion and autonomy than one finds in the typical committee.

As you read this book, look for new ways to lead your ministry. I have divided my discussion into three sections to help you. In Section I I discuss the power of the ministry-team concept and the issues involved in transitioning a church to a team-based approach. In Section II I discuss the elements involved in beginning a ministry team. And in Section III I discuss the specifics of ministry-team life.

As you move toward embracing ministry-team life, pray for wisdom and vision. Talk with others. Invite people to share your vision. Then "be strong and of good courage, and do it" (1 Chron. 28:20, KJV).

*   *

I am thankful for the loving encouragement I have personally received from each of the many ministry teams I have been blessed to be a part of, and for the continuing support of my wife, Ann Marie. I am very grateful to the wonderful Pleasant Hills Community Presbyterian Church for giving me the opportunity to write this material. I am also deeply indebted to Sam Eerdmans for giving this material an opportunity to serve the church, and for the continuing delight of working with my editor, Mary Hietbrink, as well as with my assistants, Linda Stout and Diane Davis.

Shifting to a Team-Based Ministry

What an exciting time this is for the church. In the midst of all that's changing in American culture, countless congregations are beginning to shift from long-established practices and embracing new and exciting forms of ministry. During the latter part of the twentieth century, traditional church ministry amounted to "program maintenance" — running last year's programs over again — while huge changes in popular culture were transforming the American way of life. Today many exciting new developments are bringing genuine transformation into the life of the church as it re-engages the culture with the gospel of our Lord.

In one of the most significant of those developments, congregations are moving from committee-based, status-quo organizations to team-based ministry, from leadership that is primarily concerned with task accomplishment to leadership that develops its people as well as pursues its vision.

Beginning this process is the subject I address in this opening section. In Chapter One I discuss many of the specific reasons that ministry teams are such powerful means of ministry. In Chapter Two I outline the key components of team-based ministry. And in Chapter Three I address some of the issues a leader of a congregation or ministry faces in moving a committee-based ministry in the direction of teams.

Discovering the Power
of Ministry Teams

Imagine what would happen if the following began to grow systematically in your congregation or ministry:

- The genuine experience of Christian fellowship — *koinonia*
- Growth in discipleship
- Development of new leadership
- Continuity of leadership within ministries
- "Permission-giving" leadership
- People mobilized for ministry
- Growth in interpersonal ministry as well as program-based ministry

The power of ministry teams lies in their potential to make all of these things happen in your congregation. While serving on ministry teams, I have formed many of my dearest friendships, received encouragement in my walk with Jesus Christ, and been equipped to serve and sent to lead. Just think of a ministry in which face-to-face fellowship, spiritual-gift deployment, interpersonal ministry-skill development, leadership expansion, and discipleship growth are all rolled into one experience. A ministry team does all of this while simultaneously accomplishing its vision or task in ministry. For this reason, ministry teams are among the most efficient and effective approaches to ministry available to us today.

I essentially stumbled into my first real ministry-team experience. While attending Purdue University as a graduate student, I heard about a place called the Natural High Coffeehouse and dropped by to see what was going on. I discovered that the coffeehouse was in an old, converted storefront and used large wooden spools discarded by a power company as tables. A group of college and high-school students were conducting a very effective ministry to the street kids of the day, reaching them with the Good News about Jesus Christ, growing them as disciples, and sending them to offer ministry to others. I was so inspired by their vision that I joined the coffeehouse team. That's how I came to know an amazing group of people. David Stockment had a great passion for preaching. His brother, Rodney, was an encourager with a big heart who radiated a tremendous warmth to all he met. Kevin Ball was a wonderful guitar player who became our lead musician. Brenda Kessinger (Nuland) brought vision and energy to every gathering.

Certain characteristics marked the group — characteristics that I now know are typical of healthy ministry teams. We shared a vital faith in Jesus Christ, a common vision (reaching young people), and a passion to accomplish that vision. Each of us possessed different spiritual gifts and competencies to contribute to the team. We experienced Christian *koinonia* fellowship and became dear friends. All of us grew as disciples and learned something about the art of leadership. What I experienced in that group has had a major influence on my lifelong practice of ministry, yet none of us had any formal training in ministry at the time. God simply worked through the power of the ministry-team concept itself to give us the heart for ministry and the skills necessary to accomplish it.

Huge reservoirs of service and leadership wait to be tapped in virtually every congregation. Some time ago I conducted a survey that asked every person in a congregation to identify his or her particular ministry in the life of the church. To my surprise, a great many people said their ministry was "to give money." They saw themselves as "program attendees" and "ministry receivers" — spiritual consumers who expected to get something in return for their financial commitment. They understood the "ministry" of church members to be "helping the pastor with his ministry" or occasionally holding a church office such as that of elder or deacon, or fulfilling classic service assignments such as that of Sunday School teacher, usher, youth advisor, or committee member. Eighty percent of the people didn't see themselves as having a personal ministry.

This traditional view of ministry has many positive aspects, to be sure. But ultimately it is a limited view. When a congregation begins to shift to the ministry-team concept, people start to develop new vision for ministry and to discover their own passions and gifts. They shift from a consumer orientation to one of service.

American culture is infused with team language and team thinking. The word "team" comes from Old English and refers to the harnessing of two or more animals to pull a load. It is an image that still comes readily to mind when we think of a team of oxen pulling a plow or a team of horses pulling a wagon. "Team" occurs only a few times in English translations of the Bible and is found only in the Old Testament.[1] In each case the Hebrew word indicates a yoked pair or team. Ministry teams harness us, yoke us, join us together to accomplish ministry. The concept of team also resonates with the New Testament concept of *koinonia,* the "missional fellowship" that centers on Jesus Christ and seeks to fulfill his mandates and his mission.

Biblical Pictures of Team Ministry

The Bible paints many marvelous images of team life. For the ultimate picture of a ministry team, we need look no further than the Trinity: the Father, Son, and Holy Spirit.[2] The members of the Trinity share a common vision for ministry. They enjoy fellowship in wonderfully loving relationships. And each member of the Trinity has a unique "task" or role in the process known as salvation history. They are the quintessential fusion of relationships and work — *the* missional fellowship.

Jesus and the Twelve offer another excellent picture of team life. United in the purpose of following Jesus, in fellowship, and in the ministry to which he called them, each of the disciples carried out the par-

---

1. See Isaiah 21:9; Micah 1:13; and Jeremiah 51:23.

2. The notion of the Trinity as a paradigm for ministry is developed extensively by George Cladis in *Leading the Team-Based Church* (San Francisco: Jossey-Bass, 1999), and by Miroslav Volf in *After Our Likeness: The Church as the Image of the Trinity* (Grand Rapids: Eerdmans, 1998).

ticular tasks assigned to him by Jesus. The Apostle Paul clearly led team-based ministries. I have always loved Luke's description of those who traveled by ship with Paul to Jerusalem: "He was accompanied by Sopater son of Pyrrhus from Berea, by Aristarchus and Secundus from Thessalonica, Gaius from Derbe, and by Timothy, as well as by Tychicus and Trophimus from Asia" (Acts 20:4, NRSV). I call them "The Magnificent Seven." What a team they were! United in Christian faith and committed to spreading the gospel, each one of them served in a specific role, using his particular gifts while encouraging the others in the faith.

One of my favorite biblical illustrations of team life is captured in two short comments — one from Jesus, the other from the Apostle Paul. Jesus said, "Take my yoke upon you and learn from me, for I am gentle and humble in heart, and you will find rest for your souls. For my yoke is easy and my burden is light" (Matt. 11:29-30). We take on the yoke of Jesus by faith and so are joined with others who serve him — a team. Paul pleads in his letter to the Philippians, "Yes, and I ask you, loyal yokefellow, help these women who have contended at my side in the cause of the gospel . . ." (Phil. 4:3).[3] We are yoked to other believers in loyalty, friendship, and service. Yokefellows are "teammates" pulling a common load in service to Christ — a great picture of a ministry team.

Indeed, Paul often referred to his fellow workers, his fellow soldiers, and his fellow prisoners, as well as his "yokefellow." In every case, the word we translate as "fellow" is the Greek word *sun*, meaning "with." These were the people *with* whom Paul served, who were "with" him in work, "with" him in struggle, and "with" him in friendship. This is the very essence of team. I call this the "with me" principle.[4]

Significant ministry takes a team. Jesus Christ led several teams, including the twelve apostles, the "inner three" (Peter, James, and John), "the seventy-two" (Luke 10:17), "the women" (Mary Magdalene, Johanna, and Susanna), and a family: Mary, Martha, and Lazarus.

---

3. The Yokefellow Movement, under the leadership of D. Elton Trueblood, drew its inspiration from this text, becoming a major force in the last quarter of the twentieth century in raising the banner of the ministry of every believer.

4. See my book entitled *The Joy of Discipling* (Grand Rapids: Zondervan, 1989). It is currently available from www.vitalfaithresources.com.

Think of Moses with Aaron and Miriam. Consider David's mighty men as a team, Elijah and Elisha as a team, and Paul together with Timothy and Silvanus as a team. The encourager, Barnabas, led a team in Antioch with Simeon, Lucius, Manaen, and Saul. Whatever sort of ministry you undertake — whether it be a ministry to an entire congregation or any ministry of worship, teaching, fellowship, or outreach — you will be most effective if you do it with a ministry team.

The Ministry Team:
More than a Committee with a New Name

A ministry team describes a particular way of patterning our life together in order to grow in faith, experience Christian fellowship, and accomplish a ministry vision. A ministry team is more than a committee with a new name. It is a new or more complete way to do ministry — or, perhaps more accurately, the recovery of an ancient pattern of ministry.

Conceptually, the ministry team is somewhat more complex than the committee. The designation "committee" originally meant those persons to whom a trust or charge was *committed*. In current usage, a committee is a group of people who are responsible for taking action on a particular matter. In a similar way, a ministry team is committed to take action on the vision entrusted to it. But a ministry team also develops its experience of Christian fellowship (*koinonia* fellowship) as well as the discipleship of its members. A committee rarely makes these matters of deliberate concern.

When Jesus visits the home of Mary and Martha, we discover Martha is a bit anxious because she is left with all the work while her sister seemingly "just" sits at the Lord's feet. When Martha complains to Jesus, he observes that she worries about so many things, and that Mary has indeed chosen what is better. Nevertheless, we notice that it is Martha who has opened their home to Jesus in hospitality in this story, and it is Martha who first went to Jesus to plead on behalf of her brother Lazarus. So we realize that Martha loves her Lord, and she loves people too, but she has permitted her work and her busyness to take precedence over her relationship with Jesus. Sometimes when we serve on committees and in various other service organizations, we also find ourselves so focused on the work that we pay little conscious attention to the development of true Christian fellowship among those with whom we are serving.

My friend Chuck Miller, a pastor and an educator, says, "We must *be* the people of God before we *do* the work of the people of God." Ministry teams combine the being and the doing aspects of Christian fellowship. It's not unusual to discover committees, boards, and staffs spending just a few minutes on brief devotions and then getting right to work. A friend of mine told me that he liked to get committee meetings over with as quickly as possible so, as he phrased it, "I can get back to my life." The beauty of ministry teams is that the team experience of friendship and fellowship is such that its members don't feel that their meetings are interrrupting their lives. Instead, each member can say, "The team has become a *part* of my life. I have dear friends on the team, and we have something significant to do. I belong here."

In their book *The One-Minute Manager Builds High-Performing Teams*, Ken Blanchard, Donald Carew, and Eunice Parisi-Carew make distinctions between the task functions and the maintenance functions of a group: "*Task functions* are behaviors which focus on getting the job done. . . . Group *maintenance functions* focus on developing and maintaining the group's harmony and cohesiveness. They include recognition, listening, encouraging participation, conflict management, and relationship building."[5] Effective teams have always attended to the development of team members and team cohesiveness as well as to task accomplishment. Indeed, such teams understand that the most effective task accomplishment comes as a result of team cohesiveness and team-member development.

Roberta Hestenes clearly expresses this in her excellent, succinct book entitled *Turning Committees into Communities:* "Transformed committees can be a meeting place for both relationally and programmatically oriented people. . . . My bottom line is this: Biblically, God has called us to be in some kind of Christian fellowship. Fellowship is the gift of God *and* a human responsibility by God's grace and power. The universal community of faith takes form concretely in local congrega-

---

5. Ken Blanchard, Donald Carew, and Eunice Parisi-Carew, *The One-Minute Manager Builds High-Performing Teams* (New York: William Morrow, 2000), p. 69.

tions, which are called to share together in ways that bear witness to the love and mercy of God."[6]

Ministry teams consciously practice the New Commandment — "to love one another" — while simultaneously accomplishing their vision.

The Power of Ministry Teams

Ministry teams are exceptionally flexible, dynamic means of aligning people for effective ministry while providing ongoing encouragement to each person. In effect, they are the confluence of purpose-driven ministry and small-group life. The power of the ministry team resides in the many additional benefits to those normally experienced in a committee-based organization.

The Power to Build Fellowship

God intends Christian fellowship to be one of the great benefits of participating in the Kingdom of God. "We proclaim to you what we have seen and heard, so that you also may have fellowship with us. And our fellowship [*koinonia*] is with the Father and with his Son, Jesus Christ" (1 John 1:3). This *koinonia* — Christian fellowship — intertwines our relationship with our Lord (discipleship) and our relationships with one another (fellowship).

The intensity and intimacy of personal friendships increase as the size of the group decreases. Meetings with five hundred or five thousand people can be wonderful for teaching, worshipping, providing inspiration, and generating enthusiasm, but they are less effective in developing genuine friendships. In smaller groups of less than, say, fifteen people, we discover that we most deeply know others and are known. The early church experienced this "large group–small group

6. Roberta Hestenes, *Turning Committees into Communities* (Colorado Springs: NavPress, 1991), pp. 13-14. See also Charles M. Olsen, *Transforming Church Boards into Communities of Spiritual Leaders* (Herndon, Va.: The Alban Institute, 1995), and Jessie Schut, *Beyond the Agenda* (Grand Rapids: CRC Publications, 1999).

balance." Thousands responded to the preaching of Peter on the day of Pentecost. At the same time, the book of Acts reports, "Every day they continued to meet together in the temple courts. They broke bread in their homes and ate together with glad and sincere hearts" (Acts 2:46). So, if we want our ministry teams to experience genuine *koinonia* fellowship, team life will need to have a small-group, face-to-face dimension. Indeed, ministry-team life and small-group life are inseparable. Small groups are small enough to allow everyone who wishes to speak to do so, secure enough to permit people to speak about matters genuinely on their hearts, and intimate enough to foster close relationships among virtually all of the team members.

Growth in *koinonia* fellowship occurs when the ministry team engages in corporate spiritual disciplines such as Bible study, shared meals, and prayer. People discover that they have a place to belong, others to love, and a task to accomplish — all of which are signs of true *koinonia*. Team members eat together, go to the movies, play golf, share family time, or do whatever they like to do together, and they are there for each other in times of distress. They not only know one another's names; they invest themselves in one another's personal lives.

The Power to Foster Discipleship

The ministry team consciously fosters discipleship in the lives of its members. Team life creates a culture in which growth in the spiritual life is expected and embraced. The team engages in Bible study and prayer when it meets. Team members covenant with one another to practice personal spiritual disciplines such as daily Bible study and prayer. The practices of small-group life that build fellowship — Bible study, prayer, shared meals, and shared work — are also the means of grace that develop disciples.

For many traditional congregations, the major responsibility for the ministries and programs designed to develop "spiritual growth" rests with the Christian education committee or discipleship "department" and is shared to some degree with the pastor(s). This has the effect of delegating discipleship development to a few people and ministries, while giving other church groups and programs the impression that they are primarily task-oriented and have little responsibility to develop the discipleship of their members.

For example, a traditional Sunday School committee may spend the first few minutes reading a Bible passage or sharing a short devotional, but the press of the agenda quickly moves the committee on to its primary business: the discussion of the issues facing the Sunday School, reports by department coordinators, and the assignment of new tasks and due dates. Although some attention may be paid to specific issues of the spiritual nurture of children, the traditional Sunday School committee rarely spends time discussing ways to develop the spiritual life and depth of those *on the committee itself.* The same thing happens with typical Christian education committees, stewardship committees, evangelism committees, and so on.

Because each ministry team is a center of Christian nurture as well as of service, the proliferation of ministry teams in the life of a congregation de-centralizes responsibility for the development of discipleship and spreads it around. Pastors and specialized ministries of discipleship continue to play pivotal roles in Christian nurture, but the extent to which the congregation fosters discipleship is no longer limited to the energy and scope of their efforts. Every new ministry team adds a new discipling center within the congregation.

During the second half of the twentieth century, the church had the luxury of involving people in multiple weekly activities, and almost no one thought anything about the amount of time involved. In our present over-busy age we can no longer assume that people will give this kind of time — but neither is it necessary for them to do so. Since the ministry team is both a discipling fellowship and a serving fellowship, busy people may grow in Christ *and* serve in ministry without having to attend separate meetings for each activity.

The Power to Develop Leaders

Most congregational ministries simply deploy leaders ("Get that new couple. They'll make great high-school advisors!"). Ministry teams develop and deploy leaders. Good leadership involves such a variety of behaviors that genuine leadership development is a very complex undertaking. Larry Donnithorne, President of Colorado Christian University, provides an excellent discussion of leadership in his book entitled *The West Point Way of Leadership*. He says, "Learning to lead is every bit as complex as learning to become a mature productive adult all over again."[7] It is indeed a complex matter to have the will and the skill to clarify a vision, connect people to that vision, and identify their individual roles in accomplishing that vision while attending to their needs and developing them as people. Typically, church "leadership training" often ignores that complexity by trying to develop leaders through a series of classes or officer-training events with titles such as "Leadership in the Bible," "Ministry Leadership Seminar," and "Great Leaders of the Church." Such classes can certainly provide counsel and encouragement to developing leaders, but people rarely learn to lead in a significant way by attending a class. *People learn to lead by leading.* There is no substitute for this. You have to get in the water to learn to swim; you have to bait a hook to go fishing. To learn to lead, people have to begin to lead, and in that way they will learn more about leadership.

The ministry team creates the perfect context in which people may learn to lead by leading. The team leader is assisted by a leadership core, consisting of two to four people. They learn about leadership in these supporting roles. In turn, they involve others in the accomplishment of the team's vision. Team members given particular tasks, whether major or minor in scope, learn to pull others along in order to accomplish their tasks and in so doing also learn to lead.

The ministry team becomes the consummate opportunity for leadership development in the church because it blends at least three different leader-developing processes into a single composite entity. The first such process is the small group that gathers for Bible study, personal sharing, and prayers. This is consistently one of the most prolific forms of leadership — and discipleship — development in the church. A second leadership-development process is that of apprenticing. The team leader has a few people assisting in the team leadership core for the primary purpose of teaching, modeling, and coaching them to become leaders in their own right. These are the Peter, James, and John of the

7. Larry R. Donnithorne, *The West Point Way of Leadership* (New York: Doubleday, 1994), p. 7.

Twelve. A third process is the use of "with me" ministry that emulates the pattern of Jesus Christ: offering ministry *to* people *with* people. Whenever Jesus ministered to individuals or crowds, his disciples were there *with* him, learning to become people of faith and vision, learning how to minister to people.

Ministry-team life captures all three approaches to leadership development. Team members experience small-group life, they function as apprentices to the leader, and they experience "with me" ministry.

The Power to Provide Continuity of Leadership

One of the biggest challenges in church life is the matter of succession in leadership — discerning and installing the replacement for someone who leaves a leadership position. I began my ministry in the church as a ministerial assistant given primary responsibility for a Sunday School involving several hundred children. Solo teachers, working alone, only occasionally with an aide, taught virtually every class. When a teacher gave up teaching because of a move out of town or a change in life direction, I would go through an anxious time trying to recruit a replacement from the congregation. Virtually everyone resisted the invitation to teach, knowing perfectly well that under the existing system it meant working alone with no end in sight. Only after learning the pattern of ministry-team thinking did I discover that teaching teams not only permitted the teaching load to be shared but also developed a cadre of teachers who provided a continuity of leadership. If a teacher left, there were others who could take her place.

We commonly see ministries being led by just one person. It's not unusual to discover a Sunday School class with one teacher who handles all of the administration and teaching, a children's choir with one director doing everything, a social event for which all arrangements are made by one person, and so on. People do this because they have a passion for their ministry — or because they haven't figured out how to delegate and share the workload.

This creates several potential problems for church leaders. First, in the absence of a leadership team, the ministry leader serves until he or she moves away, grows tired of the ministry, or grows old and literally cannot do it anymore. Second, when one person is the lone leader, the scope of ministry is limited to the energy level of that individual. Third, the sole leader who "does it all" denies others the opportunity to use their spiritual gifts and to serve. Fourth, no one is prepared to assume the leadership of the ministry when the present leader steps down. When the solo leader of a ministry leaves, a kind of panic ensues as others, often members of the church staff, cast about for a new leader. There is no one on the bench ready to step up and lead. Finally, the ministry, though perhaps served well by one dedicated person, lacks the energy, love, vision, and follow-through that an entire team can offer.

Some time ago, I knew a warm-hearted and hospitable person who personally called on all of the visitors to his congregation's worship services. He did this for a period of several months, but when he stopped, the visitation ministry stopped. I have also seen a congregational small-group coordinator run the small-group ministry by herself, out of love for small groups. When she quit in order to pursue another endeavor, the small-group ministry immediately began to lose momentum. The ministry team remedies this vulnerability of solo leadership in its very "team-ness." This insulates the ministry from leadership loss when a current leader steps down. Others within the team or the team's leadership core are then ready to step in, and the team experiences continuity of leadership.

The Power to Mobilize People for Ministry

The power of ministry teams rests in their success in mobilizing ordinary people for ministry. The vast majority of church members haven't come to terms with their call to ministry, their gifts for ministry, or their opportunities for ministry. This isn't surprising when we take a look at church history. By the end of the second century, church organization and ministry were increasingly centered on pastors and other key church leaders. The core biblical concept of the priesthood of all believers — the idea that every believer has a God-given ministry — was superseded by the notion that the church leaders did the ministry and the people received it. Those attitudes have certainly continued to the present day and are clearly prevalent in many traditional congregations.[8] But now a new wind is blowing. Greg Ogden describes it clearly in his book *The New Reformation*:

> The New Reformation seeks nothing less than the radical transformation of the self-perception of all believers so we see ourselves as vital channels through which God mediates his life to other members of the body of Christ and the world. . . . We are finding that in God's design all the people in the church are gifted for ministry. Ministry is not to be equated with what professional leaders do; ministry has been given to all God's people.[9]

The concept of the ministry of every believer has several implications. First, God gifts every Christian for service: "But to each one the manifestation of the Spirit is given for the common good" (1 Cor. 12:7). God has something he wants to do through every one of us! Second, that ministry is born of a serving heart: "Just as the Son of Man did not come to be served, but to serve" (Matt. 20:28a). Many times in life we are asked to assume a role or take on a responsibility in ministry for which we do not feel particularly gifted, but we do so out of a passion to serve. Third, ministry is first of all a lifestyle to be lived, not merely a program to be run.

The growing emphasis on the discovery and deployment of spiritual gifts might give one the impression that all ministry is gift-based. I would rather say, "All ministry is service-based and is the work of the Holy Spirit." Some of that ministry will be gift-based, and for that we rejoice. But sometimes we serve where we're needed, even when we have no particular passion or giftedness for the task, because at all times our ministry is rooted in a serving heart. The power of a ministry team is to encourage the development of that serving heart as well as the growth of ministry skills.

The team leader and team life work to give each person specific assignments appropriate to his or her gifts, passion, and willingness to

---

8. See Williston Walker, *A History of the Christian Church* (New York: Charles Scribner's Sons, 1970), p. 81.

9. Greg Ogden, *The New Reformation: Returning the Ministry to the People of God* (Grand Rapids: Zondervan, 1990), pp. 12, 22.

serve while offering training, coaching, and encouragement. Many church members are not mobilized for ministry because they have never received appropriate training, or because they have been asked to accomplish some task and agreed, only to find it literally dumped on them. "Will you teach the fifth-grade Sunday School class? You will? Fantastic! Here are last year's notes. See you!" I call that the "dump and run." It demotivates rather than mobilizes people for ministry. Ministry teams offer ongoing training that motivates and mobilizes.

Finally, ministry teams mobilize people for ministry by motivating them to pursue their own dreams and ideas for ministry. Teams provide built-in encouragement. They inspire a mutual clarifying of vision among the members that enables them to accomplish far more than if each team member tried to go it alone. "Two are better than one, because they have a good reward for their toil. For if they fall, one will lift up the other; but woe to one who is alone and falls and does not have another to help" (Eccles. 4:9-10, NRSV). That's team!

The Power to Accomplish Ministry

Ministry teams do share one major dimension in common with committees: they exist to get something done. Today we see many kinds of teams in our culture — athletic teams, research and development teams, marketing teams, management teams. They all center on the work to be accomplished. Ministry teams are no different. Ministry teams are missional: they have a mission to accomplish. They organize for ministry, and they are clear about their purpose and vision. They know their defining vision and practices, they organize their members according to gifts and abilities, and they measure their success by evaluating their effectiveness in accomplishing their vision.

But effective ministry teams add a significant component to their ministries, a component often missed by the more task-oriented committee, board, and task-force structures. Teams focus on both people and program (task). I call that the *double focus of ministry* because the team has one eye focused on the people to whom it is in ministry and the other eye focused on the program to be accomplished.

Making the Transition to a Team-Based Church

The traditional church in America uses a committee approach to ministry leadership. What I call transformational churches mobilize their members for ministry by embracing a thoroughly team-based approach to ministry. In a transitional congregation that shows honor to its traditional past while embracing a new transformational vision for ministry, you will find both committees and ministry teams operating side by side. The committee style of leadership continues to function while more and more people begin to experience and embrace the team approach.

New people entering a transitional or transformational congregation's life have their own preconceptions about how to accomplish ministry, ideas based on previous experiences with other churches and other organizations. Frequently their only experience has been in committee-based ministry. They have to be brought up to speed on team-based ministry and see how it functions — see how it differs from traditional committee-based work. To develop and sustain a team-based ministry throughout the ministry structure of the congregation requires constant coaching, teaching, and review of ministry-team concepts.

How long does transition take to occur? The answer is "It depends" — it depends on the commitment of pastoral leaders and other key leaders to shift to the ministry-team concept. It depends on the people available to provide leadership. It depends on the "lightness of foot," the ease with which a particular congregation adapts to new ideas. In established congregations the transition may occur rather broadly across the entire church ministry via a clearly understood strategic plan implemented with plenty of training, encouragement, and patience. A traditional congregation will most likely shift to team-based ministry via an intentional progressive transition that takes place over several years. As those who grasp and embrace the ministry-team concept move to adopt it, others, preferring to retain their existing ministry and leadership styles, will continue on their original path. New congregations and ministries can build the team concept into the "DNA" of their organizations from the very beginning.

Conclusion

Some good material is beginning to be published describing team-based ministry.[10] We need a whole lot more. The term "ministry team" is rapidly spreading throughout church organizational structures and ministries. Sometimes the term is used to rename existing ministry entities — the outreach committee becomes the outreach ministry team, the church staff becomes the staff team — yet without much change in the internal dynamics of those renamed groups. As I mentioned earlier, a ministry team is more than a group with a new name. The ministry team is a distinct leadership and ministry entity that aims to nurture its own fellowship and discipleship while serving the people and the task to which it has been called.

Ministry teams are not reserved only for pastors and church staff members or for the leaders of parachurch ministries. They are for anyone and everyone in the congregation. Ministry teams may lead entire congregations. They may lead large-scale and small-scale ministries to groups of men, women, couples, singles, youth, and children. They may be responsible for specific tasks such as ushering, snow removal, stewardship development, choirs, and praise bands. They may lead outreach ministries — a soup kitchen ministry, a Habitat for Humanity ministry, a ministry to at-risk children, an international ministry of compassion and evangelism, and so on. Whatever your ministry vision or responsibility may be, you can organize a ministry team to address that vision with you.

I want to encourage you to develop a ministry team for whatever ministry you serve or lead while also thinking through how you will begin to introduce the concept to the wider congregation. Begin to think about ways to shift committees and other task-oriented groups to a pattern that can provide richer, life-transforming experiences for their members.

In the pages ahead, I will describe ways to develop a team that attends to its own *koinonia* fellowship and the spiritual development of its members while engaging in the fulfillment of its vision. The power

10. For a thorough listing of material on team-based ministries, see the "Resources" list at the back of the book.

of ministry teams rests in the growth of their participants as disciples of Jesus Christ (as well as the expansion of opportunities for spiritual growth throughout a congregation), the deep Christian fellowship experienced on the team, the development and continuity of leadership, and their effectiveness in mobilizing ordinary people for ministry.

CHAPTER TWO

Understanding the Key Components
of Team-Based Ministry

Imagine an entire team-based ministry or congregation in which a team leads every organized ministry and in which people who undertake new ideas automatically draw a few others alongside to join them. Imagine a congregation in which choirs, classes, fellowships, and service organizations are all led by teams, where everyone knows they are gifted and sent to ministry, and others of like heart are serving with them. This is certainly possible. Whether you pastor a congregation or lead a specialized ministry inside of a congregation's life, you can begin the process of transition to a team-based ministry.

To do this successfully requires a thorough understanding of the key components of team-based ministry.

What a Team-Based Ministry Looks Like

It is essential to understand what team-based ministry looks like, especially within the larger context of a congregation. In what follows I will be highlighting four key features.

The Ministry of Every Believer Is a Defining Practice

A defining practice describes an essential aspect of personal or congregational lifestyle and gives definition to what we do. For example, prayer is a defining practice of a growing disciple. It is important to create an atmosphere in which people understand the ministry of every believer as a defining practice, both in interpersonal ministry to others and in the use of spiritual gifts in service. The concept of the priesthood of all believers (1 Peter 2:9) reminds us that ministry is a lifestyle to be lived by all of us and is not reserved only for pastors and other leaders. This defining practice offers basic preparation for team ministry because team members understand that interpersonal ministry and task assignment are both fundamental to team life.

Team Ministry Is a Defining Practice

When Ron Galvin and the First Presbyterian Church of Lee's Summit, Missouri, decided to move toward team-based ministry, they realized that their congregational by-laws, standing rules, and practice of ministry followed the more traditional and hierarchical approach. A visionary group of forward-looking individuals, each with sound credibility within the congregation, were asked to think through the implications of adopting a team-based approach. After reviewing the literature on the topic and having numerous conversations with congregational members, they proposed a completely new approach to ministry organization. While retaining key administrative elements required by their denominational polity, they placed every ministry under the leadership of a ministry team, found a way for the teams to communicate with the congregation's leadership board, and provided a means by which a person with a new dream for ministry could begin a new ministry team.

The Lee's Summit congregation moved deliberately and decisively in the direction of team ministry. Even though the structural changes were put in place fairly rapidly, this congregation has entered into a transition that will take years for everyone to understand and adjust to.

In their book entitled *Leading Congregational Change,* Jim Herrington, Mike Bonem, and James H. Furr assert, "The first key is to make a personal commitment to teams. This is not a trivial decision. Change leaders should expect resistance to team learning. Some people do not believe that a team will outperform a collection of individuals. Some find the team approach too time-consuming. They see the extra time spent in meetings and in new learning but not the benefits. Others find that the open, transparent environment of a team is too risky. They do not want to expose their thinking. Change leaders should examine their own attitudes and assumptions about teams. Before starting down that path, they should consider their own comfort with the level of interaction and disclosure that is required."[1]

Wayne Cordeiro of the brilliantly team-based New Hope Christian Fellowship in O'ahu, Hawaii, says emphatically, "You never start a ministry without a team."[2] A new ministry receives the go-ahead only when the team is in place to begin it. This means no new ministry begins unless the leader is identified and at least one other person — preferably two or three other people — are on board with the leader. This will be a change for established churches, in which people who assume responsibilities tend to carry them out by themselves. But it is a change that will reap significant benefits. This is the "with me" principle and team ministry in action.

Sending Teams Is a Defining Practice

A team-based ministry sends entire teams to accomplish specific ministry visions. To me, a congregation that understands itself as a team-sending ministry is like an aircraft carrier. The carrier launches one plane, and as that plane continues to fly, the carrier launches another and then another. After a congregation launches one team into ministry, it proceeds to launch more and more teams. This means an ever-increasing scope of effort and an ever-increasing number of people drawn into ministry. When sending teams becomes a defining practice, a congregation no longer recruits a willing individual to undertake an assignment alone. It works to help that willing person get a team together — which could be as small as three people, but a team nevertheless — and it sends *the team* rather than the individual to take on the ministry assignment.

1. Jim Herrington, Mike Bonem, and James H. Furr, *Leading Congregational Change* (San Francisco: Jossey-Bass, 2000), p. 133.
2. Wayne Cordeiro, "Building Fractal Teams," a speech given at the New Century: New Church Conference held in Palm Desert, California, in 1999. Cassettes of the speech are available from the Leadership Training Network; contact them at www.ltn.org.

Every Team Is Centered in the Defining
Vision and Practices of the Congregation

Every team will have its own defining vision, the central reason for which it organizes: to develop a discipling ministry to youth, to teach the third-grade Sunday School, to grow disciples and meet needs of working women, and so on. Such teams will also develop certain ways of going about their work, what are called their defining practices. The team that serves within a larger ministry or congregation also centers on the defining vision and the defining practices of that ministry or congregation.

A defining vision is a congregation's most central vision; it clearly and distinctively delineates what the ministry seeks to accomplish by means of its defining practices. Although "vision and values" are common terms for the way a congregation may express its core aims and convictions, I prefer to speak of defining vision and defining practices. Defining practices suggest not only that this vision is significant to us (a value), but that it is something we actually keep in mind in the shaping of ministry. For example, the defining vision of a congregation and its various ministries may be "To glorify God by making disciples and meeting human need." A truly team-based congregation functions out of a theology of ministry that thinks in terms of its vision and practices *before* designing specific activities.

If a soup kitchen's defining vision is to feed the hungry and its sponsoring congregation's defining vision is "to make disciples and meet needs," then the soup-kitchen team will pay attention to ways it can grow the discipleship of those whom it also serves soup.

One way to center every team in the defining vision and practices of the congregation is to employ the "Seven Threads of Ministry-Team Relationships." I explore these more fully in Chapter Seven, but I think it will be helpful to outline them briefly here:

> Thread One: Spiritual Disciplines: The team engages in the disciplines of the Christian faith along with congregational leaders.
> Thread Two: Face-to-Face Relationships: The team sustains friendships with congregational leaders and with other teams.
> Thread Three: Confidentiality: The team respects the confidences of others.

Thread Four: Communication: The team communicates directly and thoroughly with congregational leadership as appropriate.

Thread Five: Clear Expectations: The team clarifies its vision, objectives, and timelines and coordinates its plans with the appropriate congregational leaders.

Thread Six: The "Loose-Tight" Principle: The team serves with the freedom to fulfill its defining vision while remaining within the boundaries of the congregation's defining vision.

Thread Seven: Loving Loyalty: The team has the freedom to express its ideas and concerns with others within the congregation while supporting the congregation's ministry outside the life of the congregation.

How Congregational Leadership Supports Team Ministry

The governing authorities of the congregation bear ultimate responsibility for the ministry of a particular church. In traditional church organization, they operate in a hierarchical manner, supervising the ministries of the church. In making the shift to a team-based congregation, they retain all of their responsibility for congregational oversight while at the same time granting their various ministry teams much more independence of action. Such a shift, of course, relies on mutual trust and a clear understanding of the congregation's vision.

Think about the exciting growth of the church in Antioch after it was founded by Christians scattered after the stoning of Stephen. The mother church in Jerusalem heard about it and sent Barnabas off to investigate. When Barnabas arrived and witnessed the exciting growth, he didn't say, "Wait a minute. You didn't ask the mother church for permission." Instead, he saw the evidence of God's grace and was glad. Not only that, but Barnabas settled down there and began a teaching ministry — without seeking the official permission of the mother church. Barnabas had been sent, and he knew he already had their blessing. The members of the mother church could trust what he did because they knew that he shared their defining vision for ministry. They also knew his maturity and judgment were sound.

How do congregational leaders specifically support this kind of ministry? Let's look at several key ways.

They Develop a Permission-Giving Attitude

Leaders of established congregations often favor retaining control, maintaining the status quo, and micro-managing with a preference for developing decision-making strategies rather than disciple-making strategies. This is not to say that congregational leaders shouldn't exercise their authority and make decisions. Indeed, that is their responsibility. The issue is the attitude and style with which these functions are carried out. Is the board philosophically a "maintenance board," trying to keep the ship on its present course with little interest in the initiative and visions for ministry that others may have? Or is it a "loose-tight board," one that freely supports as many new initiatives in ministry as there are people with ideas and energy to propose and pursue them (loose), while asking that these new initiatives be centered on the congregation's defining vision and practices (tight)?

When the ministry or congregation is permission-giving, then its inclination is to "just say yes" when a new ministry proposal is introduced.[3]

They Embrace Higher Levels of Sending

One way to grasp the "loose-tight" concept in this matter of permission-giving is to think in terms of levels of sending. The lower levels exercise tighter control, while the higher levels loosen up considerably. I've identified six levels of sending:

Level 1: We tell you what to do.
Level 2: You ask us what to do.
Level 3: You ask us for permission to do what you want to do.

---

3. For more information on permission-giving ministry, read the excellent book by William M. Easum entitled *Sacred Cows Make Gourmet Burgers* (Nashville: Abingdon Press, 1995).

Level 4: You act on your own but inform us immediately.
Level 5: You act on your own and inform us routinely.
Level 6: You act on your own.[4]

In a ministry that functions at the first (lowest) level of sending, no ministry begins unless the leader or leadership board comes up with the idea and authorizes it. If a congregation operates with the third level of sending, which is very common in hierarchically organized congregations, then an individual or a committee with an idea for ministry must first get it approved by the ruling board or someone in authority. For example, if the Christian education committee wants to begin an after-school program, they will come to the ruling board and ask for permission to do it. The board will typically want to "study" the proposal for a while, and after some discussion and modification, it will approve the proposal. Ironically, the word *committee* originally described those to whom a trust or charge was *committed*, yet traditional committee-based congregations may be inclined to operate at the third level of sending because of a lack of trust and a need to regulate.

I spoke with a youth pastor recently who wanted to replace the worn, stained carpet in the youth room. He had the money in his budget to do it, he told me, but the Christian education committee to which the youth ministry reported had to approve it, as well as the building and grounds committee, their subcommittee on church decor, and the congregation's ruling board. Talk about suffocating initiative!

If a board or leadership team has "loosened up" considerably, then it regularly uses the fifth level of sending — act on your own and keep us posted. When leadership uses the higher levels of sending, they give people increasing freedom to act independently. It is similar to the situation in which we parents find ourselves: when our children grow up and leave home, we move from telling them what to do to blessing them as they make their own decisions. Jesus did that with the Twelve when he said, "As the Father has sent me, I am sending you" (John 20:21).

When a ministry acts at the sixth and highest level of sending, its affiliate ministries and its members know they have the freedom and

---

4. See my book entitled *Twelve Dynamic Shifts for Transforming Your Church* (Grand Rapids: Eerdmans, 2002), p. 76.

permission to take action as long as that action is within the bounds of the defining vision and practices of the congregation and demonstrates fiscal responsibility. For example, if the children's ministries team wants to begin an after-school program, they will just do it, centering the new ministry with the congregation's defining vision and practices while demonstrating sound monetary procedures. They will update congregational leaders concerning their progress when appropriate. Of course, should the board have any concerns or recommendations, it can easily make them to the team. However, in deference to its spirit of permission-giving, the board will keep its input to an absolute minimum, because it already accomplished one of its key roles when it established the defining vision and practices for the overall ministry. (In the rare situation in which a team acts in an inappropriate manner, the board always has the authority to intervene.)

For a congregation to operate consistently at the fifth or sixth level of sending requires trust on the part of church leaders and thoroughness of preparation and sound wisdom on the part of the ministry teams. The congregational leaders of a team-based church trust the teams to honor the congregation's defining vision and to inform them about their activities as necessary. When the team consists of mature team members who have shown themselves to be people of initiative, good judgment, and good work, it becomes a joy to bless them at the highest levels of sending.

One way for a governing board to sustain a commitment to permission-giving is to make a formal decision on an annual basis that re-affirms the defining vision of the congregation and sends the various ministry teams to accomplish their vision as long as they sustain congregational vision and stay in touch with the board. In essence such a decision says, "Don't ask us for permission. You have permission. Pursue your ministry. Please keep us informed and let us know if there are ways that we can support your work."

One issue that may influence the level at which a team is sent is the amount of risk posed to the congregation if the ministry fails. Those of us who have lived within hierarchical ministries have to resist the inclination to assume that there is real "risk" with every new ministry. By and large, we need to let God's people go and treat them as the adults they are. If they fail, they can re-group by God's grace and try again. For example, if a proposed ministry will begin a visitation to shut-ins, the risk to the congregation will be low, and the team can be launched at the fifth or sixth level of sending. There may be more actual risk associated with a new soup-kitchen ministry.

If the risks of a proposed ministry truly are significant, congregational leaders may want to carefully assess the maturity, initiative, abilities, and experience of the people leading the team before deciding what level of sending to use. And sometimes this kind of assessment will need to be made midstream. One of the short-term mission teams in my church found itself in an unanticipated and dangerous situation in which lives were at risk. This ministry, which had previously operated at the fifth level of sending, was scaled back to the third level until risks to the team could be more adequately assessed and appropriate protocols to ensure reasonable safety could be put in place. As soon as those protocols were set, the team again enjoyed the higher levels of sending.

At times a team that is very excited about its particular vision can become less sensitive to wider issues and to the feelings of those who are not as involved. A while back the church I serve introduced a major shift in one of the worship services — away from more traditional music to a much more contemporary format. There were some who really wanted to push the envelope all the way all at once. They were "enthusiasts" whose inspiration we didn't want to diminish. At the same time, it was necessary to give this team some guidance so that those who were less enthused could have the time they needed to adjust. When teams undertake ministries that involve such risk or change, then excellent people skills and sound judgment become essential to the success of the ministry and the well-being of the congregation.

A leadership board concerned with the leadership readiness of a new team or the risks associated with a new ministry may practice progressive sending. It may "send" the new team initially with the third or fourth level of sending and move to the sixth level just as soon as the new ministry gains experience and grows in effectiveness. Generally, people have more vision and initiative than we give them credit for. So it is usually wise for leaders to start at the highest level of sending they can and give the team a chance to make its own way.

Of course, leaders don't actually say things like "You may act at the sixth level of sending" or "We're scaling you back to the third level."

They simply use the levels as guides to help them think about how closely they need to oversee a given team's ministry, stepping back as much as possible and stepping in only if need be. The goal is to spend less time supervising and more time envisioning and ministering, to send at the highest possible levels to increase the opportunities that ministry teams have to creatively conceive and initiate ministry.

No matter what the "risk" of a new ministry may appear to be, or whether the congregation or ministry is more hierarchical or decentralized, basic to sending ministry is the matter of trust, as mentioned before. As a congregation moves in the direction of team-based ministry, the teams are trusted to act at the highest level of initiative and wisdom.

They Give People the Freedom to Initiate Ministry at All Levels

In a team-based ministry, congregational leaders work to develop vision and initiative at all levels of the congregation. Groups and individuals throughout the congregation are encouraged to envision and initiate new ministries. If a pastor has a heart to see a new ministry of compassion grow, if a congregational member has a passion or an interest in developing a ministry to small business owners, both are encouraged to identify and invite team members and launch teams.

In the traditional congregation of the last fifty years, a new ministry usually began when the pastor or staff member recruited someone to organize and launch the ministry. More often than not, a pastoral staff person or an elder or deacon would actually be that organizer/launcher or would sit in on all of the meetings. Such a system ensured stringent accountability to the governing board. It also limited the number of new ministries to the energy level of the pastor and leaders and, not surprisingly, led to a lot of exhausted church people.

In a team-based congregation, the freedom to initiate new teams is the province of the central leadership *and* the participating ministries *and* members within the overall congregation. So leaders of the congregation are free to initiate new ministry by conceiving vision and then finding suitable leaders who invite teams and launch ministries. Clearly there are core ministries within every congregation — ministries devoted to worship services, teaching, caring, small groups, outreach, finances, and overall management. These ministries are essential to sustain the congregation and allow it to flourish. At the same time, individual participants or various teams within the congregation who come up with ministry ideas on their own are also encouraged to put a new team together and get going. Such a structure retains overall order and direction while granting great freedom to initiate throughout the congregation. It decentralizes initiative while it maintains the centralized defining vision and practices.

Tom Bandy discusses the different approaches to launching ministry today in his book entitled *Coaching Change*. "Consider a common congregational dilemma like the need to initiate a new outreach mission," he says. "How will we do it?"

- The pre-modern answer: Let's get an authority from the home office to tell us how to do it!
- The modern answer: Let's hire a professional to do it for us!
- The post-modern answer: Let's build a team and turn them loose![5]

Team ministry is rooted in the idea that every member is gifted for ministry (Ephesians 4) and is to be invited, equipped, and sent with others to accomplish ministry. The "language" of team ministry is filled with questions: "What are your spiritual gifts?" "What is your ministry?" "Who are you in ministry to?" "With whom are you in ministry?" Every question is designed to give people a vision for their ministries and those with whom they will engage in ministry. The language of sending to ministry will saturate sermons, other teachings, newsletters, and interpersonal conversation in the team-based ministry.

When a congregation promotes initiative at every level, it becomes a permission-giving, deploying, "sending" ministry. The central leadership of the congregation does everything it can to encourage its teams and its members to act with the highest level of initiative and asks only to be kept informed. Policies are reduced to a minimum. Congregational and ministry-defining purposes and practices are spelled out clearly and briefly so that they can be used practically as a benchmark for every team's ministry.

5. Tom Bandy, *Coaching Change* (Nashville: Abingdon Press, 2000), pp. 75-76.

What Key Linkages Nurture Team Ministry

The opposite of organization is chaos, with its resulting confusion, disarray, and disorder. In true chaos there is no principle of relationship, order, or organization to bring true cohesion among individuals — it's everyone for themselves. Obviously the successful accomplishment of any vision will be jeopardized by true chaos. But, by taking into account key relationships or linkages to the wider organization when "sending" others, chaos can be eliminated and the potential for success and further growth maximized.

A new team may be launched by an existing team as one of its affiliate teams, or by the leadership team of the congregation, or by an individual with a dream for ministry. In every case, there are a variety of potential linkages between the new team and the overall ministry that are important to discuss here.

- The key linkage in team-based ministry is a team's commitment to the defining vision and practices of the congregation or ministry. Once that is in place, a team has a reference for both the boundaries within which they work and the freedom they have to initiate. Three years ago my wife, Ann Marie, and I sent our daughter Shelley with the sixth level (act on your own) to Vanderbilt University, where she is now a junior. Would you believe that she rarely calls home asking for permission to do something! I don't worry about her either, because I know that in the eighteen years she lived with us she learned the defining vision of what it means to be an Ott as she absorbed our family vision and practices.

  Recall the freedom the mother church gave Barnabas when he was sent to Antioch. Although the book of Acts mentions no formal decision-making process between Barnabas and the mother church, there is clearly a strong linkage between Barnabas and the leaders in Jerusalem. The application is clear: When a team is grounded in the defining vision and practices of the congregation, and there are trusted relationships between them and congregational leaders, then that team will operate within the framework of congregational vision without requiring close supervision.

- Another important linkage is that of a ministry team to a daughter team it has launched (subordinate to the originating team or parallel to it) to accomplish a particular vision. The originating team invites, equips, and sends the new team leader and offers ongoing support to his team.
- A useful means of linkage is the "VHS" (Vision, Huddle, Skill) format introduced by Carl George.[6] Team leaders and their leadership cores periodically meet with other leaders for a brief word of vision (lifting up defining vision and defining practices), "huddles" (breaking into small support groups led by "coaches"), and skill training in some facet of team leadership. Such "VHS" groups can meet weekly, monthly, quarterly — at whatever frequency best serves the ministries involved. Getting team leaders together and occasionally getting all teams and team members together helps them see that what is happening is bigger than they are, and it gives them the opportunity to exchange ideas and provide encouragement.
- Another key linkage may be provided by a coaches ministry team. Each coach has about five ministry teams to whom he or she offers counsel and encouragement, while providing a direct link between these teams and congregational leaders.

As Glenn McDonald, pastor of the Zionsville Presbyterian Church (Indiana), puts it, "Leaders of a Church in the Spirit must also choose to be *accountable to other leaders.* The community is healthy when its leaders are in healthy community with God and with each other. To be a small group or ministry leader means to enter a relationship with a lay or pastoral coach. The coach arranges regular meetings in which to listen, encourage, and advise the leaders under his or her care . . . , and to watch each leader's heart monitor for God."[7]

Periodically these coaches meet in their own ministry team to share experiences and encourage each other.

- Another fundamental linkage is that to staff member/elder/deacon. Staff members and/or congregational leaders may be "contact

---

6. Carl F. George, *Prepare Your Church for the Future* (Old Tappan, N.J.: Revell, 1991).

7. Ben Campbell Johnson and Glenn McDonald, *Imagining a Church in the Spirit* (Grand Rapids: Eerdmans, 1999), pp. 128-29.

people" for teams, acting as coaches who provide counsel, encouragement, and a linkage with the governing bodies of the ministry. As the number of teams grows, the function of the staff members and congregational leaders changes: they no longer directly supervise but act more as liaisons through whom the teams keep the central leadership team/board informed of their work. Teams do not report *to* them so much as *through* them, keeping the central leadership team informed.

The board members also become less involved in direct supervision or specific program management. Their role becomes more visionary in character: they work with staff to discern the direction the Spirit is leading the congregation and respond to the various issues that arise. As a ministry becomes increasingly team-based, there may be more and more teams that have no direct reporting liaison to the board. They act on their own and sustain their linkage with the larger ministry by adhering to the congregation's defining vision and by receiving guidance from their team coach when the team leaders meet together. (Obviously, the board has the authority to step in any time that it becomes concerned, but this happens rarely in a healthy team-based ministry.)

Organizationally, team-based ministries are "flatter" than traditional ministry structures. For example, in a traditional organization, each elder or deacon on the board is responsible for a program or a committee. So there is an elder who chairs the Christian education committee, an elder who leads the stewardship committee, and so on. This makes for a "high" hierarchical structure. A team-based ministry functions very differently, and as the number of ministry teams in a congregation begins to proliferate, it is no longer possible — or necessary — for staff, elder, and deacon-level leaders to offer direct leadership or supervision of every team. Members of the congregation's leadership board become liaisons for entire "families" of ministries in order to give those ministries access to the board as needed. The board offers little direct leadership or supervision of those ministries. The organization is "flat" in that each member of the board or leadership team can be the liaison for ten, twenty, or more different groups rather than having the "span of control" of five to seven groups that defines classic hierarchical organization. While the board retains overall authority, the ministry is increasingly decentralized as the people of the congregation are invited to initiate ministry in accord with congregational vision and practices.[8]

Congregational leadership must communicate clearly how those who want to begin new ministries get started. Every potential ministry founder would be invited to receive training and encouragement in ministry-team leadership practices and receive any necessary assistance in establishing the proposed new ministry-team activities in accordance with the congregation's defining vision and practices.

Conclusion

While ministry teams are more the exception than the rule in established congregations today, many congregations are moving to embrace this exciting approach to leadership. Understanding the key components of team ministry brings a congregation one step closer to making a team-based ministry a reality.

8. For a balanced approach to decentralized congregational ministry, see Ben Campbell Johnson and Glenn McDonald, *Imagining a Church in the Spirit*.

CHAPTER THREE

Modeling the Way

As James Kouzes and Barry Posner point out in their very helpful book, *The Leadership Challenge,* leaders are to model the way. "Leaders go first. They set an example and build commitment through simple, daily acts that create progress and momentum. Leaders model the way through personal example and dedicated action. To model effectively, leaders must first be clear about their guiding principles. Leaders are supposed to stand up for their beliefs, so they better have some beliefs to stand up for. Eloquent speeches about common values aren't nearly enough. Leaders' deeds are far more important than their words and must be consistent with them."[1]

Leaders model the defining characteristics of their ministry that they want to inspire within every facet of the ministry. If interpersonal ministry with others is a defining practice, then the leaders model it. If small-group life is a defining practice, leaders are involved in small-group experiences.

If you want your ministry to be a team-based ministry, you will have to model it. If you encourage others to use the ministry-team format but continue to use old patterns to lead the board, staff, and other leadership entities in a strictly task-oriented committee format, they will only do as you do.

This is true regardless of the size and scope of the ministry you lead. You say, "But in a larger ministry, fewer people have the opportu-

---

1. James M. Kouzes and Barry Z. Posner, *The Leadership Challenge* (San Francisco: Jossey-Bass, 1995), p. 13.

nity to directly observe the leadership style of the leader and leadership core." Perhaps so, but those few who do observe your approach to team-based leadership will model it to a great many others. Furthermore, even if you're leading just a single ministry team, you're going to be wrestling with the real issues of team life: issues of inviting and recruiting people, of forging team fellowship, of equipping team members and discerning their serving roles, of leading the "thinking ahead" process, of resolving conflict on the team, and of launching affiliate teams and sending people to serve. You are going to be making personal friends on your team and seeing teammates grow in discipleship and in excitement and effectiveness in their ministries. Being immersed in such an environment, you will automatically speak of facets of team life in teaching or preaching, in newsletters and in private conversations. If you are experiencing team life, you will model team behavior in every other facet of the ministry.

Becoming a Team-Based Leader

The activity trap easily captures us in this busy age. Ministries get caught up running the same activities, the same program year after year, making few adjustments for changing needs and opportunities. In precisely the same way, pastors and ministry leaders get caught up in their particular style and approach to leadership and the deployment of people in the organization of ministry. Shifting to a team-based approach to ministry, therefore, first requires a shift in the leader's approach to ministry. Leaders who want to see others "do team" have to "do team" themselves.

This can mean a significant change in leadership style for a person who has been leading in a traditional church. In this context we learn well the lessons of committee-based leadership and micromanagement, in which pastors and other leaders often expect to have a hand in every decision. Ministry teams are potentially much more complex entities than committees, and the experience of learning to lead them and participate in them is crucial for leading an entire congregation in a shift to a team-based ministry.

Following the Steps to Transition to Team-Based Ministry

Following several basic steps can facilitate the transition to team-based ministry.

First, communicate the vision for teams throughout the congregation. Have conversations beginning with key decision-makers and moving outward in concentric circles to include more and more congregational leaders and participants. Such conversations may occur in the context of retreats, workshops, and the studying of printed materials. Communicate the philosophy of team, the implications of becoming a team-sending ministry, and the training to be made available on an ongoing basis.

Second, lead the congregation's leadership board to understand and then endorse the defining practice that all new ministries will be team-based. When someone proposes a new ministry, he will be "sent" to begin that new endeavor only when he has others on board with him in a ministry launching team.

Third, model team life as both a staff and as a congregational leadership team.

Fourth, establish a "ministry team ministry team" to lead the transition.

Additional steps you may take to introduce the ministry-team concept to your congregation or to your ministry include the following:

- Build twenty minutes of "small-group life" involving Bible study, sharing, and prayer into every committee or appropriate group meeting in the congregation or ministry. (See Chapter Seven for details.) When a group numbers more than fourteen, have people break into groups of four to six for this time of sharing, which will automatically begin to build fellowship. (Exceptions to this would include monthly fellowship dinners, worship services, and other gatherings in which an extra time of what I call "Word-Share-Prayer" would be more of an intrusion than a help.)
- On an ongoing basis, bring before the congregation the teachings of Scripture and stories of people's experiences concerning team ministry, every-member ministry, and small-group ministry.
- Conduct ministry-team training sessions using materials like this book for those involved in existing leadership and ministries. Give

guidance to those who are starting new teams or transitioning existing ministries with the team-based approach.

Leading the Transition

To move to a team-based ministry takes intentional leadership. Form a "ministry team ministry team" as a transition team whose role is to assess the potential of the team-based future of the congregation and who will provide the strategy and good-spirited leadership that will be required. Take an inventory of all of the task-oriented ministry groups, committees, boards, and staff that your ministry presently has. Consider the particular people leading those groups, their flexibility and openness to change, their experience in small-group life and in interpersonal ministry. Develop a progressive plan to lead every willing committee and leadership group to a ministry-team format.

Greg Warner, writing in the online magazine FaithWorks.com, touches on some of the issues involved in leading a congregation in transition from a committee-based to a team-based ministry:

> George Bullard, director of New Reformation Solutions,[2] says adopting team leadership requires "a significant cultural shift" for churches. "Many pastors, staff members and long-term lay leaders will never have functioned in a team-based church," says Bullard of Columbia, S.C. "They will have trouble even conceiving how it will work. Some laypersons, particularly persons who have been members of the church for more than twenty years, may resist a move to team-based ministry," he adds. "They will feel a loss of accountability, a loss of their position of hierarchical authority in the church, and a loss of commitment to the denominational way of structuring a church." Still, he notes, with careful coaching, it can happen. "This is an opportunity to help them learn about ministry in a postmodern context. It is also an opportunity to help them see the New Testament in a new light."[3]

2. Bullard is with the Hollifield Leadership Center (http://www.hollifield.org). He is associate executive director of the Baptist State Convention of North Carolina.

3. See http://www.faithworks.com/archives/power_teams.htm.

The critical question is one of leadership: how to bring people along to a new way of doing things and how to keep them with you. Invariably, some committees and work groups will have been together for so long that they won't want to change their approach to leadership and ministry. Whether it is wiser to let them be or to insist on change (at whatever pace) is a judgment call. I myself don't believe that it's wise to impose a team format on a committee that really isn't interested in changing. Shifting to ministry-team life means adding new depths of fellowship and discipleship as well as considering the implications of the double focus of ministry (people and program). Such shifts may be more than an existing group wants to engage in. I say, Bless that group! Express appreciation for their service while simultaneously turning your attention to those groups whose members are amenable to shifting to the team format. Over time, those who have had healthy ministry-team experiences will permeate all congregational organizations, and the shift to a team-based church will continue to develop.

It is far easier to make the ministry-team shift with people who have experienced small-group life, because the small-group experience is essential to growing disciples and developing friendships among team members. Such people understand what small-group life and interpersonal ministry are all about. Where small-group experience is foreign to the majority in a particular group, simply proceed at a pace they can handle. Don't ask for or expect in-depth Bible study or deep sharing of personal lives or everyone praying aloud. On the other hand, don't hesitate to *lead* the committee-turned-team in a simple "Word-Share-Prayer" format. Over time they will "get it," and it will grow on them and nurture their experience of fellowship. Suggest that they share meals together about three times a year in a restaurant or someone's home. Or you may simply say, "Next time, let's meet a little earlier and order in a pizza and 'break bread together.'" In addition, help the members form monthly prayer partnerships.

Remember that the people focus of team ministry isn't commonly part of committee life. People typically join committees to accept a task assignment. So, in the beginning, encourage the committee-turning-into-a-ministry-team to engage in interpersonal ministry just within the comfort zone of the team members. Begin with something everyone can do, such as praying for the people they serve by name. By involving them initially in interpersonal ministry that suits their level of readiness, you will be able to guide them along the ministry-team path.

Being Alert to the Issues of Transition and the Tactics of Change

As you begin the transition, have the image of team-based ministry and the defining practices essential to its success clearly in mind. And be prepared for the impact the transition will have. As William Bridges puts it, "The single biggest reason organizational changes fail is that no one thought about endings or planned to manage their impact on people. Naturally concerned about the future, planners and implementers usually forget that people have to let go of the present first. They forget that while the first task of *change management* is to understand the destination and how to get there, the first task of *transition management* is to convince people to leave home. You'll save yourself a lot of grief if you remember that."[4] So begin by knowing where you're going before you begin to convince people to "leave home."

Many of the attitudes that tend to hinder new ministry-team initiatives are centered in control issues. Remember that older congregational structures tend to focus on boundaries. Congregations that want their members to conceive, launch, and participate in ministry teams must more readily grant the freedom to initiate when it comes to program and activity, while requesting that those ministries be centered in the defining vision and practices of the congregation.

Adults handle change in a variety of ways. Some, seeing the opportunities, welcome change or at least don't mind it. Others see all change as loss and react the way any of us do when losing something we value — by grieving or getting angry. If making the change is difficult in your particular situation, be present, affirm, and don't argue — listen. And use a strategic transition process such as the "The Eight-Stage Process of Creating Major Change" introduced by John Kotter:

1. Establish a sense of urgency
2. Create the guiding coalition

4. William Bridges, *Managing Transitions* (Reading, Pa.: Perseus Books, 1991), p. 32.

3. Develop a vision and strategy
4. Communicate the change vision
5. Empower broad-based action
6. Generate short-term wins
7. Consolidate gains and produce more change
8. Anchor new approaches in the culture[5]

The transition team working to lead the congregation to a team-based ministry has to start with the matter of urgency. Established churches have typically run a board-centered, committee-based ministry for a long time in which the only people considered responsible for interpersonal ministry are pastor, staff, and specially trained members. As Kotter explains, "Establishing a sense of urgency is crucial to gaining needed cooperation. With complacency high, transformations usually go nowhere because few people are even interested in working on the change problem. With urgency low, it's difficult to put together a group with enough power and credibility to guide the effort or to convince key individuals to spend the time necessary to create and communicate a change vision."[6] It's been said that change happens in response to "a burning ship or a compelling vision." Essential to transition to a team-based ministry is that congregational leadership become so convinced of the value of the team concept that they communicate it and continue to communicate it with the passion that a compelling vision demands.

It takes time to move a more traditionally organized congregation to a team-based ministry in which the majority of teams are led by members of the ministry and not solely by elders, deacons, and pastors. It also takes time to instill the vision among congregational members that ministry initiative is not the sole responsibility of pastor and officers. During the period of time that the church is a "transitional" church, a mix of old and new attitudes and structures will simultaneously exist. Committees and ministry teams will work side by side. Some leaders may lead committees. Others will encourage entire fami-

5. John P. Kotter, *Leading Change* (Boston: Harvard Business School Press, 1996), p. 21. Another wonderful resource for leading change is Spencer Johnson's *Who Moved My Cheese?* (New York: G. P. Putnam's Sons, 1998).

6. Kotter, *Leading Change,* p. 36.

lies of ministry teams. Use the "bless and add" philosophy. Bless existing ministries that choose to remain in their current organizational approach. And add new ministries. Require them to be team-based, of course, but offer them all the support and encouragement they need to succeed.

Encouraging

Even with the best of motives, people who have spent much of their adult life in ministries that are high in task focus and low in direct interpersonal ministry and small-group life will need encouragement as they transition to a team-based system. Given the tension that can exist between individualism and team collaboration, even the most experienced team leader can find herself seriously challenged to sustain team spirit and motivate the team to accomplish its vision. Look for a variety of ways to encourage teams and their leaders, from one-on-one conversations, to a gathering of team leaders, to an entire grouping of teams, to public encouragement from pulpit and platform. Look for ways to acknowledge the dignity and honor of those who serve on teams. Let them know they are sent to serve with blessing.

At the same time, be encouraged yourself. Changing to a team-based ministry may require many changes in your personal style of ministry and in your approach to organization. As with any new undertaking, there is a learning curve, and part of the adventure of ministry is experiencing both success and failure, learning from both, and moving forward by faith. Team up with someone you know who is doing team ministry elsewhere so that you can give each other mutual support. Ask questions. Express frustrations. Share ideas. Be encouraged!

Loosening Up

Essential to team-based ministry is the ministry's affirmation of a basic team covenantal agreement: "Loose-Tight" — we serve with freedom and within boundaries. The congregation that shifts to team-based leadership learns to give its teams genuine freedom to initiate as long as those initiatives are congruent with the congregation's boundaries of defining vision and practices. Two things are involved here. First, the defining vision has to be clear, and the defining practices sufficient to guide teams without overly restricting their freedom to initiate. Second, the leaders have to learn to "loosen up," to personally exercise the defining practice of "sending teams" and empowering them to do their work.

Pastors and leaders of ministries can be remarkably "tight" (even uptight) in their leadership and management styles and feel it is both their right and their responsibility to exercise a high level of control. However, they can certainly permit trustworthy, faithful people to initiate new endeavors with considerable freedom without diminishing their responsibility for oversight. A team-based church decentralizes initiative throughout the church without abridging the congregational leadership's responsibility for such oversight. So, be "tighter" when exercising greater presence and influence in the determination of defining vision and practices, and be "looser" in blessing teams to find their own way to go about their work.

Daniel Reeves makes the point clearly for pastors: "Be prepared to make major adjustments in your pastoral style. The shift from being a directing pastor to being a coaching pastor will need to be negotiated and reinforced along the way. It usually takes a minimum of 12 months to fully make the transition. A common struggle for pastors in the initial shift is the tendency to keep a tighter rein than most teams are comfortable with. There is widespread reluctance by clergy to share responsibility. The number-one reason for this is fear that the job won't be done correctly."[7]

Letting go of this fear is key to "loosening up."

Balancing Focus on Team Members and Teams

In her incisive book entitled *Connective Leadership,* Jean Lipman-Blumen sums up one of the contradictions in American society succinctly: "We preach teamwork, but we idolize individualism." She observes that we

---

7. R. Daniel Reeves, "Practical Advice for Launching Teams," *Ministry Advantage* 8, no. 1 (Winter 1998): 2.

"genuflect before the concepts of cooperation, teamwork, and the rule of the majority. In reality, cooperation and teamwork serve mostly as the backdrop for individual performance." She points out that a related contradiction is that our individualism "is often incompatible with the human institutions in which we inevitably live." She writes, "We teach our children to be individuals, to face their own problems, to set their own goals, and faithfully devote themselves to these isolating tasks until they have painstakingly met their own exacting standards. At the same time, we expect them to join groups that call for collaboration, cooperation, *inter*dependence, negotiation, and persuasion."[8]

I believe it is essential for us to take Lipman-Blumen's observations into account in moving to a team-based ministry. The established church has traditionally furnished a backdrop for the star performer, and we give disproportionate honor to those whose work is highly visible, disproportionate deference to the most vocal person. The ministry team must give each team member an avenue to fully express his abilities and initiative while at the same time retaining overall team cohesiveness and good spirit. This is again the double focus of ministry applied to the team itself, a focus that neither places the individual above the team nor places the team above the individual. It's both, all of the time, because both together, the part and the whole, constitute one body. Given our penchant for individualism, the process of learning to be a team player can be a challenging one, both for the team leader as well as the team member.

Jim Herrington, Mike Bonem, and James H. Furr put it well: "By disposition or experience, many church leaders are inclined to use a 'lone ranger' style of leadership. They tend to interact with other leaders only as necessary. But leaders who generate effective change create strong teams, even when it is their natural preference to work alone. They learn how to function interdependently with others. In so doing, they are able to achieve far more than the combined efforts of a group of individuals."[9]

8. Jean Lipman-Blumen, *Connective Leadership* (New York: Oxford University Press, 1999), pp. 71, 72.

9. Jim Herrington, Mike Bonem, and James H. Furr, *Leading Congregational Change* (San Francisco: Jossey-Bass, 2000), p. 98.

Leaders who would fashion genuine ministry teams face the challenging task of motivating every individual while simultaneously keeping everyone centered on the team experience. The goal of service has to be balanced with the goals of discipleship and fellowship. This may prove quite challenging, but with the investment of sufficient time and resources, it will bear great fruit.

Molding the Staff into a Team

Program staffs work with and carry out policies and program initiatives by leading many activities and ministries. In many traditional ministries, such staffs function internally with a task-oriented committee design, and they can be very effective in deploying their members to areas of responsibility. When a staff itself makes the shift to the ministry-team model, it improves not only its own "quality of life" but also its effectiveness in ministry. It goes beyond its usual focus on program assignments. It learns to pay deliberate attention to its own fellowship (through "Word-Share-Prayer," prayer partnerships, shared meals, and covenantal agreements) and to practice the double focus of ministry by attending to the exercise of interpersonal ministry as well as programmatical assignments. Since staff members lead various ministries, when they practice team life they function as models who can teach others how to "do team" in their respective ministries.

Unlike the typical ministry team, a staff team will carry additional responsibilities and confront certain issues because they are participating in a team as part of their employment.[10] Nevertheless, they will exhibit all of the essential facets of ministry-team life. And when members of a staff team are enjoying friendships with other team members, being encouraged in their own faith and faithfulness, and relishing the challenge of their ministries, their attitudes will be infused throughout the entire congregation.

10. There are many excellent resources that you may use to develop your staff team. See, for example, George Cladis, *Leading the Team-Based Church* (San Francisco: Jossey-Bass, 1999); Jon R. Katzenbach and Douglas K. Smith, *The Wisdom of Teams* (New York: HarperCollins, 1994); and Gary L. McIntosh, *Staff Your Church for Growth: Building Team Ministry in the Twenty-First Century* (Grand Rapids: Baker Books, 2000).

Taking Courage

Few things will cancel your ministry initiative more effectively than fear and anxiety. Typically, it's not the big fears that slow us but the subtle fears that pull at us, influencing us to delay or avoid taking action, diminishing our initiative as leaders. Moving people into a ministry-team approach may be very easy for you, or you may meet with some opposition. Think of the encounter between David and Goliath. You can be sure that David was afraid of the giant. But David put his trust in God and put his fear aside: "The LORD who delivered me from the paw of the lion and the paw of the bear will deliver me from the hand of this Philistine" (1 Sam. 17:37). And with God's help and just five smooth stones, David got the job done. *That's* Godly courage.

Any vision that will move your ministry team forward can inspire anxiety. If you respond to that anxiety by avoiding the vision set before you, in essence you are tempted to let fear become your vision. Fear can easily lead you to "under-plan," to aim at less than God has made you capable of simply because you allow fear to immobilize or limit your initiative.

Godly courage is the will to act that comes from faith in Jesus Christ, the will to do what must be done even though you don't feel like doing it. Three simple steps can give you courage as a team leader. First, face your fear and act in faith. I love the verse that says, "Be strong and of good courage, and do it" (1 Chron. 28:20, KJV) — whatever "it" is. Whether it is a phone call, a meeting, a confrontation, a request for help, or a change to initiate, remember to trust the Lord and do it. Trust the power of God, move out, give it your best effort, and leave the results to God.

Second, remember that you're inclined to put off the very things that you're nervous about doing. Let that very anxiety help prioritize the ministry of your team. Do first the things you fear the most, unless there are sound reasons to delay.

Finally, confess specific fears to your team. They will hold in confidence what you share, and their prayers and encouragement will hearten you. Together, with God's help, you will accomplish great things.

Vision and courage are a bit like Vitamin C. We need them in fresh doses every day. We cannot store them up. Yesterday's vision may be too small for today or simply out of touch with people's changing needs and changing ministry opportunities. Yesterday's fears may no longer bother you, but there will be new challenges that will shake your confidence. Sound leadership, like a good sprinter, runs on the two legs of vision and courage. Vision sets the course. Courage and faith give the needed power. "Have I not commanded you? Be strong and courageous. Do not be terrified; do not be discouraged, for the LORD your God will be with you wherever you go" (Josh. 1:9).

Moving to team-based ministry can indeed be a challenge. But trust God, take courage, and do it!

Conclusion

When our children were growing up, our family life was very much the life of a ministry team. My wife, Ann Marie, and I functioned as the "leadership core." We assigned each of our children specific tasks around the house that related to their ages and their responsibilities outside the home. After the family supper every Sunday night, we spent some time at the table, sharing our joys from the past week, the ways in which our Lord had blessed us. Then each of us shared personal concerns for the coming week. Finally, we held hands and prayed for one another. When there was a major task to undertake (like putting up or taking down the Christmas tree), we thought ahead together, determining who was going to do what.

Ministry-team life is family life within the body of Christ. Just as families range in cohesiveness and unity, in levels of function and frustration, so ministry teams can embrace a wide range of human experience. Shaping a vital ministry team is hard work, but the benefits are well worth it.

Recently my daughter Lindsay called me from her office in Washington, D.C., to ask a question about the family schedule. When our family gets together — my wife and I, Lee and Sophia, Lindsay, and Shelley — our first and immediate joy is the pleasure of just being together. Similarly, when team members effectively grow in fellowship, resolve disagreement, and accomplish the team's vision, there are few greater pleasures in ministry than just being with them.

This is the heartening vision that I hope will encourage you to model the way.

SECTION II

Getting the Team Together

Launching a new ministry team is an exciting endeavor because it gives you the opportunity to draw people together around a common vision and to establish the ground rules of ministry-team life right from the very beginning.

In Chapter Four I discuss the elements or steps involved in beginning a ministry team. When you look at the ministry of Jesus Christ, you can see that he used some of these elements in getting his ministry team of the Twelve established.

In Chapter Five I offer guidance concerning the team's leadership, and in Chapter Six I review the issues surrounding the identification and enlistment of the members of the team.

CHAPTER FOUR

Starting the Team and Preparing for Ministry

When my friend Tom Saxon learned of the ministry-team concept, he realized its power immediately. Tom was the director of a ninety-member chancel choir. Although such choirs often have an executive committee to handle administrative details, not many of them are led by true ministry teams. Tom began to pray through the list of his choir participants, and after a while he identified the ones who shared his heart and vision for ministry. He invited eight people to join a ministry team that eventually grew to fourteen. They began meeting every week, right before the entire choir gathered for rehearsal. They opened with a fellowship-building time of "Word-Share-Prayer," and then practiced the double focus of ministry (people and program). First they reviewed concerns for individuals in the choir and determined appropriate interpersonal ministry for follow-through. Then they reviewed the various administrative and choral assignments of the team members. The team gradually started five small-group Bible studies with choir members which met at different times during the week; each one was led by a ministry-team member. With the support and guidance of a ministry team, that choir became one of the most active centers of winsome discipleship and enthusiasm in the congregation.

Starting a successful new ministry team means getting the right people with you, establishing a pattern of meeting to develop team fellowship, and working to lead the ministry for which the team was called into being.

When you think about it, ministry-team life can become fairly complex. From identifying, inviting, and mobilizing the team members, to nurturing them in both discipleship and fellowship, to organizing them for ministry, there are many essential elements of team life.

Element One: Clarifying the Team's Vision

"Come follow me," Jesus said, "and I will make you fishers of men."
MATTHEW 4:19

Vision plays a major role in defining the boundaries and extent of a team's work. There are actually several facets to the overall vision of a ministry team.

Understanding the Defining Vision and Defining Practices of the Congregation

It is critical for a ministry team to understand the defining vision and practices of the congregation, which we discussed in a previous chapter.

So, if the defining vision of a congregation is simply "to glorify God by making disciples and meeting needs," then clearly every affiliate ministry team (e.g., the small-group ministry team, the youth ministry team, the women's ministries team, the soup-kitchen team) could say, "What are we doing to 'make disciples'?" "What are the needs of the people we are serving, and how can we address them?" "What more can we do, and what can we do differently to increase our effectiveness in disciple-making and in well-being?"

The same is true of defining practices. Suppose a congregation seeks to spread responsibility for Christian nurture throughout the life of the church instead of relying solely on the programs of the Christian education committee, even though such a centralized program will continue to bear fruit. Instead of parceling out the responsibility for spiritual growth to one or more program areas, the congregation's leadership makes discipleship development one of the congregation's defining practices. As a result, *all* groups — small groups, committees, and ministry teams alike — understand that they are to engage in practices that will encourage the spiritual development — the discipleship

— of the group members while simultaneously accomplishing the ministry the group is responsible for.

Bill Easum and Tom Bandy have co-authored a book in which they explore the core vision, values, and beliefs that lead to mission in a congregation.[1] Easum calls this the "DNA," the genetic code, of a congregation that shapes the life of each of the affiliate groups and activities of the church.[2] It is this "DNA" of a ministry that makes up defining vision and defining practices.

With this "DNA" clearly understood and stated, the permission-giving board then delegates broad authority to the staff and various ministry teams of the congregation. "As long as you seek to accomplish the defining vision and use the defining practices, you have our blessing to pursue your particular vision for ministry. Just keep us informed on an appropriate basis."

Vital congregations articulate clearly their philosophy of ministry, their defining vision and their defining practices. These may be gleaned from a bestseller on the subject or articulated and modified according to the congregation's own theology and understanding of ministry.[3] Only with such a philosophy of ministry may a ministry team within a congregation design initiatives that are not only consistent with but also an actual expression of the congregation's vision for ministry.

The congregation or ministry may also have some operational poli-

---

1. William Easum and Tom Bandy, *Growing Spiritual Redwoods* (Nashville: Abingdon Press, 1997). See also James C. Collins and Jerry I. Porras, *Built to Last* (New York: HarperCollins Publishers, 1994); and Aubrey Malphurs, *Values-Driven Leadership: Discovering and Developing Your Core Values for Ministry* (Grand Rapids: Baker Books, 1994).

2. Bill Easum, *Leadership on the Other Side* (Nashville: Abingdon Press, 2000), p. 93.

3. There are a variety of excellent, biblically sound philosophies for ministry being published today. Although they differ in terminology, they express many of the same principles or defining practices of transformational ministry. See Tom Bandy, *Moving off the Map* (Nashville: Abingdon Press, 1998); Kennon Callahan, *Twelve Keys to an Effective Church* (San Francisco: HarperSan Francisco, 1983); Christian A. Schwarz, *Natural Church Development: A Guide to Eight Essential Qualities of Healthy Churches* (Carol Stream, Ill.: ChurchSmart Resources, 1996); E. Stanley Ott, *Vision for a Vital Church* (Pittsburgh: Vital Faith Resources, 1994); E. Stanley Ott, *Twelve Dynamic Shifts for Transforming Your Church* (Grand Rapids: Eerdmans, 2002); and Rick Warren, *The Purpose Driven Church* (Grand Rapids: Zondervan, 1995).

cies and procedures that place certain boundaries on the work of the team. A permission-giving, "sending" congregation will minimize such policies, but some of them may be necessary for appropriate order. For example, there may be a procedure for handling money and a policy on facility use. There may be some guidelines for transportation safety during church-related activities, for the ratio of adults to youth on a mission trip, for the circumstances when liability coverage is necessary, and so on. It is important that ministry teams be fully aware of these boundaries.

Articulating the Unique Defining Vision of the Team

In the top-down organizational structure that views all ministries in a highly controlled hierarchical relationship, from the ruling board and staff "down" to all the subordinate ministries, ministry vision and initiative often begin with the congregational leaders' senior team, its board and staff. In a team-based church, some teams are launched to fulfill ministry aims of the senior leadership team, while other teams are begun by people who have their own visions for ministry. Members of the congregation are invited to dream their own dreams for ministry and to invite others to join them on ministry teams to accomplish those dreams as long as each team heeds the defining boundaries of the congregation. For example, someone may say, "I have a concern for women experiencing separation and divorce." A team would gather around that person and her vision while keeping the defining vision and practices of the congregation in mind.

New ministry may also arise from a planning process in which congregational leaders conceive of new endeavors based on a variety of factors such as biblical mandates, perceived needs and oppotunities, life stages and life situations, and personal-interest areas. If the team vision arises out of a biblical mandate such as evangelism, then the team will organize itself around specific ways to accomplish the work of evangelism. A ministry based on a perceived need might focus on those going through the pain of a divorce. A ministry focused on a life stage could be geared to people in their twenties. A personal-interest ministry might focus on those interested in learning about stained glass. Each

Biblical Mandate	Needs and Opportunities	Life Stage/ Situation	Interests
• Worship	• The sick	• Adults	• Diet
• Teaching	• Divorce recovery	• Children	• Exercise
• Discipleship	• Grief recovery	• Youth	• Travel
• Fellowship	• Shut-ins	• Working men/ women	• Sports
• Mission	• Those in need of financial assistance	• Retired people	• Technology/ Internet
• Leadership	• The homeless	• Singles	• Music and the Arts
• Evangelism	• International hunger relief	• Married couples	• Hobbies

column above offers a variety of examples of the areas from which the vision for a new ministry team may arise.

Whether the team vision arises out of a biblical mandate, need, or interest, every team organizes around a vision for ministry. Know your own team's unique vision, and be able to express it in a sentence or two. What are you seeking to do, with the help of God's grace?

"Our team vision is to develop senior high school students as disciples as we center on our congregation's vision to make disciples and meet needs."

"Our team vision is to feed the hungry by means of a soup kitchen as we center on our congregation's vision to make disciples and meet needs."

"Our team vision is to be a praise band to lead others in worship as we center on our congregation's vision to make disciples and meet needs."

State your vision succinctly, so that you may use it as a benchmark for your team's work. It will help you ask the right questions about your progress: "Are we accomplishing our vision? Why? Why not? Where do we go from here?"

Element Two: Identifying the New Team Leader
and the Leadership Core

*One of those days Jesus went out into the hills to pray, and spent the night
praying to God.*   LUKE 6:12

In reality, element one and element two are interchangeable in order. It
just depends on which comes first. If the idea for a new ministry surfaces first, then the next step is to identify the leader. If a person has a
vision for beginning a new team, her first step is to clarify the team's vision so that she may invite people of kindred spirit and like heart to
join her.

When a planning process leads to a new idea for ministry, then
those with the initial vision begin to say a prayer something like this:
"Lord, help us discern who could provide ongoing leadership to this
new endeavor. Who has a heart for this vision? Who has the will and the
skill, the spiritual gifts to lead this endeavor?" After such prayerful
searching, the leader is identified and invited to develop a team. That
leader then begins to pray about who might be invited to be a part of the
team's leadership core (and will continue to pray that "prayer of selec-
tion" as long as he or she leads the team). The leadership core consists of
two or three key people who, along with the leader, guide the team.

The qualities to look for in identifying a potential leader are much
the same as those for any team member: someone with a heart for God
who cares about and for people, someone with a passion for the vision
of the team, someone who is willing to lead others. The leader of a new
team is frequently someone who is already serving on a ministry team
and is ready to lead a team of his own. Sometimes a founding leader of
a new ministry team will not remain its ongoing leader. As the new
team assembles and the various abilities of the team members are discovered, the founder may discover that he prefers some other role on
the team and may yield the leader's role to someone else.

A new leader for an existing team ideally comes from within the
leadership core of the team. Such a person will know the vision of the
team and already be a part of its fellowship. The responsibilities of a
team leader remain the same, regardless of how he or she assumed the
role.

Element Three: Inviting the
Beginning Ministry Team Together

When morning came, he called his disciples to him and chose twelve of them, whom he also designated apostles.   LUKE 6:13

The leader invites a few others who share the vision and will join in a fellowship defined by covenantal agreements (the Seven Threads of Ministry-Team Relationships). In the early stages, the leader pays special attention to identifying and inviting those two or three others whose capabilities and interests are appropriate to the leadership core of the team. The leader makes the invitation privately, face to face, when seeking people of particular spiritual gifts, maturity, and heart. The leader makes the invitation publicly when he or she is open to being joined by anyone of similar interest who will abide by the team's covenantal agreements.

Team Size and Organization

Any two people who share a vision and kindred spirit can be a ministry team. "For where two or three come together in my name, there am I with them" (Matt. 18:20). They may be a teacher with a fellow teacher who have a vision for a class, a married couple whose ministry is their family, or two or three friends who share a ministry in their neighborhood. On the other hand, teams can grow as other people of like interest are invited to join the team.

Team size and therefore the number of people you may wisely invite to join the team is governed by a number of factors. Since the ministry team functions as a small group in its fellowship, it cannot easily exceed the normal maximum size for a small group — around fourteen people — without losing the intensity of interaction, planning, accountability, and follow-through it needs to function well. If the group grows larger than fourteen members, some form of substructuring will be necessary to permit adequate face-to-face, small-group community.

Remember, too, that teams with just four or five members can work with considerable effectiveness while experiencing deep Christian fellowship. The most effective team is never larger than the number of available people with heart for God and vision for the task. Better to have a team of five with heart than ten who don't really care, won't shoulder their share of the load, and have no vision for the people or the program. At the same time, the ideal size is large enough to accomplish or oversee the work that must be done.

There are a variety of ways to organize the team to involve all of the people interested in the ministry. Wayne Cordeiro describes the concept of "fractal" teams at New Hope Christian Fellowship in Honolulu. Each team has five members: the leader and four others, each of whom leads one area of responsibility. Each of those four in turn leads an affiliate team subdivided into four areas of responsibility. And the leaders of those four areas in turn lead affiliate teams — and so on, until everyone in the ministry participates in a team and leads a team.[4] It is a pattern similar to that of multilevel marketing, in which each person may lead a team whose members in turn lead teams and so on. It is a powerful way to develop leaders while giving everyone a place to serve and experience fellowship.

Another way to approach team organization when it has more than fourteen members is to utilize a "central ministry team," sometimes called a "coordinating" or a "master" ministry team. Such a central team will have up to fourteen members, each of whom leads affiliate teams branching off the central team. Some of the affiliate teams may in turn have affiliate teams of their own. Thus, for example, the ministry team of a youth ministry becomes a central ministry team with several affiliate teams: a retreat ministry team, a small-groups ministry team, and a Wednesday-night Bible-study ministry team.

In another arrangement, the central team and the affiliate teams all meet separately from each other except for periodic meetings in which they all gather for vision and encouragement. A helpful meeting pattern utilizes the "VHS" format I mentioned earlier. All of the teams gather for a brief time — about fifteen minutes — to discuss vision (V) with the overall ministry leader. The group then moves into the huddles (H), meetings of the affiliate teams that focus on sharing, encour-

4. Wayne Cordeiro, *Doing Church as a Team* (Ventura, Calif.: Regal Books, 2001), pp. 176-95.

agement, and prayer. Finally they regather for skill training (S) in some facet of Christian life and ministry.

If a team is larger than fourteen members, then it's best to spend the "Word-Share-Prayer" portion of the meeting gathering in small groups of four to six people before continuing on with other program matters. This ensures that everyone can experience face-to-face *koinonia* fellowship. An alternate way to do this is to have the team leader lead the large group in a short study of the Word. The group then breaks into smaller groups for "Share-Prayer."

I spoke with a friend this week who leads seventy adults in a ministry team. They meet in a large group for encouragement and vision but have little "face-to-face" time. I reminded him of the biblical principle of "large group–small group balance": Jesus addressed large crowds but also spent time with small gatherings. The book of Acts says of the early disciples, "Every day they continued to meet together in the temple courts. They broke bread in their homes and ate together with glad and sincere hearts" (Acts 2:46). They were in temple courts with the many and in homes with the few. When my friend's large team spends some time sharing and praying in smaller groups, they will be able to experience a far deeper level of fellowship.

The Next Ring Out

While I was serving a congregation near Purdue University, my wife, Ann Marie, and I began a ministry to college students. Using a central ministry team format, we led a team that in turn led twenty small groups, a large-group gathering that stressed fellowship and teaching, outreach events, and a host of other activities reaching about 250 college students. But we soon realized that God was raising up many more capable students with eyes and hearts for interpersonal and task-oriented ministries than we could ever utilize on the central ministry team. They needed to be a part of some small-group leadership team or affiliate group if they were going to continue their spiritual development and if we were going to keep them in our college ministry.

We began to imagine the total leadership of the college ministry as concentric circles, something like a doughnut — the central ministry team was the hole, and the doughnut itself we called "the next ring out." The next ring out included all willing-to-serve people who were not on the ministry team.

Identifying, developing, and deploying the people in the next ring out and engaging them in some area of service is essential to the growth and vitality of the overall ministry of a team or congregation. Involve as many people in the next ring out as you possibly can. If your team is as large it should be for effective planning and interpersonal relationships, then help others in the next ring out connect with a place to serve on an affiliate team or other related ministry teams within the overall congregation.

The more people a team can engage, the more people will be given a chance to serve Christ, and the more work will be done. For this reason it behooves the team to be aware of people in the wider ministry it serves whose gifts, interests, and hearts make them suitable to invite to the work.

Element Four: Engaging the Ministry Team in Discipleship and Fellowship

When you pray, go into your room, close the door and pray to your Father, who is unseen. Then your Father, who sees what is done in secret, will reward you.   MATTHEW 6:6

I have called you friends.   JOHN 15:15

It is important for the ministry team to begin its meetings with a time of small-group life using the "Word-Share-Prayer" sequence. When there are time pressures, fellowship should not be sacrificed for task. The team leader and leadership core carry out a double-focus ministry to the team by seeking to encourage each member in interpersonal ministry using the six defining practices for fostering discipleship (see Chapter Eight) and by developing the health and fellowship of the team as a group.[5]

5. See Appendix Two for a discussion of the frequency and scheduling of team meetings.

It is important to nurture the interaction that occurs in these meetings in other ways. Encourage team members to develop prayer partnerships. And try to schedule group meals at least three times a year. These are ways to strengthen and enrich the team's life together.

Element Five: Guiding the Ministry Team in Interpersonal Ministry and Organizing It to Accomplish Its Vision

*They came to Philip, who was from Bethsaida in Galilee, with a request.
"Sir," they said, "we would like to see Jesus." Philip went to tell Andrew;
Andrew and Philip in turn told Jesus.* JOHN 12:21-22

*Taking the five loaves and the two fish and looking up to heaven, he gave
thanks and broke the loaves. Then he gave them to his disciples to set before the people.* MARK 6:41

The team needs to be organized in such a way that it can develop its own fellowship and can engage in a double focus of ministry — to people and to program (task). The leadership core leads the whole team by teaching and modeling ways in which team members may develop discipleship and meet the needs of those to whom the team is ministering. The team also needs to be organized to accomplish its vision. The roles and responsibilities of each team member depend on the nature of this vision and the abilities of the team members.

Take a "men's outreach event" ministry team whose vision is "to win men to faith in Christ in order to involve them in the life of the church, and to send them on Christ's behalf to their families and places of employment." The team attends first to its own fellowship. Then team members engage in interpersonal follow-through ministry with the men who attend their outreach events.

Conclusion

The process of organizing a team involves a number of elements, which, though I've discussed them sequentially, often occur in an overlapping fashion. This is true because vision clarification, leadership identification and development, new team-member invitations, and discipleship, fellowship, and ministry are all ongoing processes in the life of a healthy team. Team life, like family life and the life of the entire congregation, is the group of individuals working to accomplish the tasks necessary to attain their vision while also working on the quality of their interpersonal relationships.

CHAPTER FIVE

Developing Team Leadership

When we wanted to launch a new one-to-one mentoring ministry within the overall youth ministry in my congregation, the first question was "Who should lead it?" Instead of recruiting just any eager member of the congregation, we were praying and asking ourselves, "Who has a heart for this particular ministry to children? Who has the requisite organizational and people skills?" We knew the success of the entire endeavor hinged on the person we invited to lead the team. Rose Comer surfaced as that person. As soon as she consented to lead the new team, we worked with her to identify a few more people with a similar passion for youth work and the abilities that would strengthen this emerging ministry. When we launch a new ministry, we want a sound core of leaders from the get-go. Their spirit, initiative, and capabilities will determine in large part the effectiveness of the effort.

There are a variety of ways people become leaders of ministry teams. Sometimes a leader who has a vision for a new ministry founds the new team. Often this is someone who has been serving on another ministry team and is ready to lead a team himself. At other times a specifically gifted individual like Rose is invited to lead a new team. Leaders for ongoing teams naturally arise from within the team itself. Sometimes a team leadership position comes with a church leadership position such as pastor, elder, or deacon.

Leading the Ministry Team

A basic motion of the body in all sports is known as the triple extension movement — the simultaneous extension or use of the hip, knee, and ankle. This allows for the greatest exertion of power; it helps the weightlifter heft heavier loads, the runner sprint faster, the cyclist cover ground more quickly. As I see it, ministry team life also has a triple extension movement: discipleship, fellowship, and ministry. Ministry team life is at its strongest when its missional work is enriched by "growing" disciples and nurturing fellowship among its own members.

Recall that Jesus always initiated the triple extension movement of ministry-team life. He focused on discipleship, instructing his followers both when he taught the Word to large gatherings and when he discussed the Word with them alone. He focused on fellowship, sharing meals with them, going on retreats with them, being a friend to them. And he focused on ministry, inviting them to participate in whatever he was doing at the time.

Anyone beginning a role as team leader needs a clear picture of the triple extension movement of ministry team life. We all have a tendency to repeat past ministry and organizational experiences. A great many of the participants in church life today have had some experience in committee-style leadership. They will be inclined to reproduce a committee-style meeting that bears the label of "ministry team" but doesn't develop the team's life of discipleship or fellowship. (This concept is developed more fully in Chapter Seven.)

This means that the leader must have a clear understanding that the team is not a committee, a small group, or a class — although it displays elements of all three. The leader encourages the fellowship of team life by leading the team to honor basic ground rules or covenantal behaviors. At the same time, she guides the team in a double focus of ministry so that the team attends to individual people as well as to group-related task matters. This means that the leader needs a broader range of skills than someone who leads a task-oriented committee. Like a committee leader, the team leader must have the skills to facilitate the team's thinking about its future ministry and the deploying of members to accomplish various tasks. But a team leader will also need the skills of small-group leadership and a command of the ministry practices that foster discipleship.

All of this points to the necessity for thorough and ongoing leadership training for those who are team leaders and others who are part of a team's leadership core. If a congregation is to successfully make the transition to a truly team-based ministry, it needs the leadership training to support it.

Moving from Solo Leadership to Team-Based Leadership

It is remarkable how frequently I observe ministries led entirely by one or two dedicated, often exhausted leaders who do virtually all of the organizing, leading, teaching, and detail work by themselves. Such ministries include the following:

A Sunday School class (for students of any age)
An adult evening class
A choir (of any age)
A men's breakfast or lunch
A short-term mission team
A women's Bible-study group
A singles' ministry
A Habitat for Humanity work group
A fellowship group for senior citizens or singles or youth
A sanctuary decor guild
An ushering ministry organization

The leader leads out of a passion for the ministry but leads alone because she likes doing everything by herself, has never thought of developing a ministry team, assumes that no one else will help, can't get anyone else to help, or has received no encouragement or assistance in identifying and inviting team members. No matter how effective this leader is, the impact of her ministry will be greatly multiplied by the addition of a ministry team.

In the game of football, a popular play is known as the "I" formation. The fullback lines up directly behind the quarterback — like the dot of an "i." If the fullback is good, he does most of the running for the team as the quarterback passes him the ball on play after play. Doing traditional ministry in which the leader does almost everything is like running the "I" formation.

Another popular but more complex play is called "the wishbone." Three ball carriers line up next to each other, right behind the quarterback, so that the four of them form a "T." When the ball is snapped, the quarterback can pitch it to any of these runners. A ministry team follows the wishbone formation. Instead of one over-busy person doing all the work, several people carry responsibility for people and for program. It is a more complex but potentially a much more personally fulfilling and effective way to do ministry.

If you are currently leading a ministry alone, make the development of a ministry team a top priority. Initially this will mean additional work for you, but the effort will be worthwhile. Even with the addition of just two or three others, more people will grow in Christ, develop new personal friends, and together accomplish much more than you could ever do alone. The effectiveness and impact of your ministry will multiply greatly.

Identifying the Leadership Core

Key to leading the team is sharing the load of leadership and developing other leaders. When the team is small, numbering less than half a dozen or so, the entire team functions as the core. As the team grows to between ten and fourteen, however, the leader gathers an "inner team" made up of himself and usually one to three others that function as the leadership core. They are like Peter, James, and John, the inner three of the Twelve Apostles. As Scripture says, "A cord of three strands is not quickly broken" (Eccles. 4:12).

Gareth Icenogle, in his book entitled *Biblical Foundations for Small Group Ministry*, offers an excellent study of Jesus in his leadership of the Twelve as well as the inner core:

> Leadership implies group process. If there is a leader, there must be at least one follower. Most initiatives of human leadership are ven-

tured in the context of a small group. This is because leadership requires accessibility and nearness. While there is a kind of leadership that directs crowds and large groups, it is difficult to lead well from a distance. Face-to-face connections are important for successful long-term leadership. Followers need to be able to touch and see and feel their leaders. This can happen only when a leader is close enough to be encountered and experienced. Most helpful leadership happens in the midst of small bands of followers. Leaders of large groups usually lead a small group of leaders who lead other small groups. Leadership is therefore the leading of a small group or the leading of a small network of groups. Jesus understood this basic leadership rule: lead a small group of leaders who will in turn lead their small groups of leaders, who will lead the people. . . . Leadership, to be effective, must be in the midst of a leadership community. Jesus selected and developed his own leadership community, and they changed the world.[1]

Jesus used a 12-3-1 pattern with the Twelve. He spent time with the entire team and also spent separate time with the leadership core, who were a subset of the ministry team. The Beloved Disciple, John, shared a special bond with Jesus as both apprentice and friend. The Gospel of Mark records three times when Jesus included only his inner three: when he went to the home of Jairus (Mark 5:37), when he went up the Mount of Transfiguration (Mark 9:2), and when he became distressed in the Garden of Gethsemane (Mark 14:33). Peter, James, and John were among those to whom Jesus was most fully vulnerable, the ones closest to him in the sharing of ministry. It is no surprise that they became among the most significant leaders of the early church.

The 12-3-1 pattern is useful for the ministry-team leader as well. Within a team of ten to fourteen people, one to three people will typically surface who have a more exceptional interest in the ministry, a deeper affinity with the leader, and a keen willingness to serve. When the leader identifies his "inner three," he will share deeper fellowship with them and share in the doing of ministry together as they inspire

---

1. Gareth Icenogle, *Biblical Foundations for Small Group Ministry: An Integrational Approach* (Downers Grove, Ill.: InterVarsity Press, 1994), p. 161.

one another to develop as leaders. More than likely a team leader will also discover a "John" among the leadership core, someone with whom at the deepest level he can struggle to solve new problems and dream new dreams.

In the event that the team leader is founding a new ministry, the first step is to find two or three others with a similar level of interest in the team vision whose gifts will complement those of the leader. For example, if the leader is founding a team to begin a ministry to retired men, he might look for people with organizational gifts and small-group leadership experience who are comfortable talking to people on the phone.

The leadership core is the key to the team's ongoing development of leadership. It is most likely that from this core will arise the person who will succeed the present leader or be sent to lead a new ministry team. In fact, this is extremely important for leadership development for the whole church. To fully grasp the point, consider the following questions:

If you left your ministry/program and no one was brought in from the outside to replace you, would the ministry continue with the same level of excellence?

Would the ministry you presently lead progress to new levels of accomplishment without you and without a replacement for you from the outside?

If your answer is "no" to either question, then you see immediately the value of using a leadership core as a means of leadership development.

The fascinating book *Built to Last* by James C. Collins and Jerry I. Porras is a careful study of why some corporations do very well over a long period of time and why others in the same industries flounder.[2] One of their key insights is that the corporations which flourish are those that have promoted from within. Collins and Porras discovered that those within the corporation, far from having limited vision, were capable of great vision. They also understood the corporate culture,

---

2. James C. Collins and Jerry I. Porras, *Built to Last* (New York: HarperCollins, 1994).

knew the people involved, and were best able to work within that culture to effect change and movement. When a team has an inner core and the leader leaves the team, someone from that core who understands the ministry's culture and vision will be ready to step up and offer fresh energy to sustain the team's ministry.

It's a simple but powerful truth: We learn to lead by leading. The leadership core gives individuals besides the leader the opportunity to lead — to think through the needs of the team, to help attend to interpersonal ministry needs with team members, and to assist in leading the overall team to accomplish its mission. Members of the core may also lead affiliate teams to accomplish some facet of the vision of the central ministry team.

In effect, members of the leadership core function as leadership apprentices rather than mere assistants. The apprentice has different objectives than the assistant. The goal of the assistant is to help the leader. The goal of the apprentice is to learn to lead and to work to become like the leader in terms of responsibility, wisdom, and vision. Assistants help. Apprentices learn. Assistants fill in. Apprentices take over. Assistants grow weary. Apprentices grow increasingly excited about their work.

By identifying a leadership core, the leader shares the load of leadership, develops apprentices for their future personal leadership roles, and practices leadership in the midst of a supportive community.

Using the Double Focus of Ministry

As he introduces the subject of different spiritual gifts, Paul says, "Just as each of us has one body with many members, and these members do not all have the same function, so in Christ we who are many form one body, and each member belongs to all the others" (Rom. 12:4-5). To build the body we must always attend to the "one body" — the whole body — and to each member. This means practicing the double focus of ministry described earlier — keeping one eye on each and every person and the other eye on the body (the group and its tasks). Put simply, it means retaining an emphasis on both people and program.

We read in Matthew 8 that Jesus goes to Peter's home and heals his mother-in-law. In Matthew 16 we see that Jesus praises Peter for his God-given confession that Jesus is the Christ; the next thing we know, he is upbraiding Peter for contradicting his assertion that his death and resurrection are imminent. Believe me — Peter felt the personal attention of Jesus. Yet this singling out occurred in a conversation Jesus was having with *all* of his disciples to explain what would soon happen and to call upon them to take up the cross and follow him. Jesus attended to each disciple and to all of the disciples together.

In a similar way, the ministry-team leader will be a team builder working to develop the fellowship and the discipleship of the team members themselves. The leader and the team core will be guiding the team in accomplishing the vision to which it is called. In this situation the double focus of ministry is actually used twice. First, the team leader exercises the double focus on the team itself, showing concern for each team member as well as the overall team. Second, the leader guides the entire team in its double focus on its specific ministry: both people (each participant) and program.

The Leader and Leadership Core Focus on Team Members

The team leader and the leadership core interact with team members with the goals of both ministry and modeling. In ministry to team members they serve and encourage them personally, and as they lead they model patterns of ministry for team members to use in their ministries to others.

The team leader's challenge and joy is the development of the people on the team. The team is more than a committee that gathers to divide up the work and go home. In its fellowship as well as its discipleship the team develops its people even as it accomplishes its mission. A leader takes great pleasure in seeing the people on his team growing in faith and developing in ministry effectiveness, something Paul clearly experienced in his work with the church at Corinth: "For even if I boast somewhat freely about the authority the Lord gave us for building you up rather than pulling you down, I will not be ashamed of it" (2 Cor. 10:8). Of course, building people is always a two-way experience, since we "mutually encourage" one another in our walk of faith (Rom. 1:11-

12). The team leader says, "Let's discover together what Scripture says. Let's grow in Christ together."

The leader and the core care for team members by means of the interpersonal ministry of follow-through. Jim Tozer, my friend and mentor, says that the force of discipleship is the impact of life on life. Follow-through is the specific practice of interpersonal ministry offered in response to particular situations in individuals' lives. It requires us to be alert to the things happening in the life of each team member — a new job, a sick child, an ailing parent, a significant birthday. If Paul misses a meeting, the leader or someone in the core follows through with a call: "We missed you, Paul." If Janice is having an operation on Tuesday, someone follows through on Monday — "We want you to know that we're praying for you" — and touches base again on Wednesday: "We're thinking about you." Follow-through includes prayer, care, encouragement, witness, discipling — indeed, any action designed to encourage someone's heart and faith. This follow-through expresses care for team members and also models how they may follow through with those to whom they are ministering.

The Leader and Leadership Core Focus on Team Life

Team life is the supportive community that nurtures discipleship and fellowship among team members. The leader and leadership core guide the group in the small-group practice of "Word-Share-Prayer." As the team becomes familiar with the pattern, the team leader may continue to lead the small-group portion of the team meeting or rotate the lead among team members, a strategy which has the advantage of giving everyone experience in small-group leadership.

Other facets of team life include prayer partnerships and the sharing of group meals. The core can lead these activities, although if certain team members express special interest in doing so, they may be asked to take over. The core schedules the team's planning events and fellowship retreats.

The team leader also guides the team in review of the covenantal agreements, the Seven Threads of Ministry-Team Relationships (detailed in Chapter Seven), whenever a new person joins the team or at least once every season of the year. These agreements help the team consider and grow in the depth of their fellowship. The team discusses each agreement, exploring how they are doing with each one. The team also considers what they want the nature of their life to be for the upcoming months. Such discussions are undertaken in a positive spirit, with leaders and team members alike thinking and brainstorming together concerning ways they may further shape the loving heart of team life.

George Cladis offers excellent counsel on the role of the team leader and the covenant agreements of the ministry team. He writes,

> Team covenants, too, are forged between equal partners. Each person is respected as a child of God who is gifted for service in the church. The team leader is not conceived of as a sovereign over subjects but as an equal child of God whose function is to lead through the service and the building of covenantal ministry teams. The leader's task and responsibility are not to shape the group in the leader's own image but to see that the team lives out its covenantal agreements with Christ and the congregation at large and that team members live out their covenantal agreements with one another.[3]

The team leader and the core lead the team in determining vision and the group's next steps as well as individual assignments. At the same time, the leader works to build a sense of teamwork that suggests, "We're in this ministry together." When I was leading the ministry of the Natural High Coffeehouse, which was designed to introduce high school students to faith in Jesus Christ, we used to close the doors at eleven at night. We were exhausted and more than ready to head home and go to bed — but we didn't. Instead, the team just lounged around together, reflecting on the evening's ministry: the intense home situations some of the teens were coping with, the kids who had made commitments to Christ, the sometimes unusual people who had come through the doors, and so on. We laughed and commiserated and simply thanked God for working among us that evening. This was our way of enjoying being a team together.

3. George Cladis, *Leading the Team-Based Church* (San Francisco: Jossey-Bass, 1999), p. 37.

The Team's Double Focus on Its Ministry
(the People and the Program)

In its focus on people, the team exercises interpersonal ministry with those its ministry serves and assesses the needs of those people when planning programs and activities. In its focus on program, the ministry team functions like any committee or leadership team. Guided by the team leader and the core, the team uses an intentional ministry planning process to consider its purpose, its goals based on that purpose, its defining practices, its people needs, its program design, and its organization. Just as in the committee, the ability of the team to clarify its vision and goals, to organize and delegate work, and to follow through in accomplishing that work is essential to the overall effectiveness of the ministry.

Coaching the Team

Teams today tend to be more collegial in nature, having a less top-down "do this and report back" atmosphere. Team leaders are first and foremost coaches, doing whatever equipping and encouraging is necessary to send team members to undertake specific tasks. In effect, the team leader becomes a coach of coaches as he or she coaches team members who in turn coach the people who are serving with them on affiliate ministry teams.

The basic coaching process consists of demonstrating (modeling desired behaviors), doing (having an individual practice the behavior), and reviewing (giving the individual constructive feedback and encouragement). For example, the Bible study leader leads several meetings, then an apprentice leads a meeting while the leader is present, and afterward they evaluate the experience. Or the person in charge of the prayer chain sets up a chain with the help of two others. These two are then asked to organize the next prayer-chain event. The original prayer-chain leader, as coach, offers insight and encouragement.

Suppose Jennifer, a member of a hospitality team, is asked to enlist ten people to help with a special one-day event, and she is encouraged to talk to each of the ten face to face. Instead, she sends out letters of invitation and receives only a few favorable responses. When the team leader hears about this, she realizes that Jennifer needs some coaching. "Let's you and I visit John and Mary," she says. "I'll invite them to join us. Then we'll call on Jim and Jenny, and you can offer the invitation. We can talk over coffee afterwards."

Coaching means that team members are continually developing their skills in ministry, because leaders are continually encouraging them to grow and take on new challenges.

Resolving Conflict

Conflict is a normal part of team life when people of imagination and energy see things differently. In the church I serve, there is a praise team whose ministry during worship services is greatly appreciated. During some of the team's recent conversations, there was an amazing range of opinions expressed about what music should be selected, how loud it should be, what musical instruments should be used, how to decide who would lead the team during the service, and so on. In light of the changing, complex world of contemporary music in worship, such questions are not only common but necessary.

The leader of the praise team works to preserve the cohesion of the team while at the same time letting the team grow in the way it needs to. Sometimes individuals have left the team when they no longer felt compatible with the team's direction, and others have joined the team because they did.

In such situations the leader and the core are crucial. They function as bridge-builders, as agents of reconciliation when necessary, as moderators of discussion to ensure that no one's voice is being ignored, and as decision-makers when team consensus isn't enough to resolve a particular matter. Above all, the leader works to encourage the team to live out its covenantal agreements, all of which have to do with shaping the unity and relational quality of the team so that it can be a healthy, highly functional group of people.

Showing Initiative

Initiative is the will to act, the self-starting motivation to move forward by faith. It's not enough to have vision. To lead effectively, a leader must have the motivation to move out, to make a difference, to motivate his team to accomplish its vision. As he gets to know each team member, he will also begin to understand each person's level of initiative: Tom waits for instructions, Sandy will act on her own, and so on. The team leader has two objectives here. One is to model initiative and the other is to develop initiative in team members. It's important to challenge every team member to exercise the highest level of initiative he or she is capable of showing. This recalls our earlier discussion of "loose-tight" — the balance between freedom and boundaries — as one of the team's covenantal agreements: it's key to want to grant all of the freedom possible to each team member commensurate with their initiative, abilities, and experience. The more people are free to initiate, the greater the scope and impact of the team's work will be.

The leader develops initiative by entrusting as much responsibility to individuals as they are capable of assuming and by providing support, encouragement, and a means of review and accountability. The key is coaching and feedback.

Conclusion

As I see it, every ministry team should have a clearly identified leader, someone who operates with the "inner core" to lead the team. Even if the leader encourages others on the team to take responsibility to develop fellowship and to work out individual assignments, the leader is someone who, along with the core, carries the responsibility for the overall life and well-being of the team. The leader ensures that team members have responsibilities appropriate to their abilities and situations, and he works to make them successful. The leader, along with the core, also connects the work of the team to the larger congregation and its governing board. Much is being written today about the possibilities of self-organized teams, and they are an avenue that some team ministries will want to explore. But whether leader-led or self-organized, healthy team life requires some form of leadership that pays attention to convenantal agreements and the triple extension movement of discipleship, fellowship, and ministry.

The role of the leader is to lead. This doesn't mean to dictate or dominate. Neither does it mean that the leader is only a discussion facilitator, a person who moderates or referees the discussion of others. It does mean that, along with the core, the leader communicates a vision and works to draw several individuals together into a fellowship centered on that vision. A leader leads when he motivates people to accomplish a vision, whether that vision comes from congregational leaders, the leader himself, or team discussion and times of thinking ahead. When the team is filled with highly motivated and visionary people, the leader's task is certainly simplified.

More significantly, the leader sees to it that the vision of the team is clear and that the team fulfills its covenantal agreements. The team leader works to develop the "teamness" of the team, the culture of strong relationships and good spirit that is conducive to a team life that is both passionate about its mission and effective in its work.

CHAPTER SIX

Identifying and Inviting Ministry-Team Members

One of the most significant acts of any athletic coach happens before the team even gathers. It is through the process of finding the right players to join the team that much of the team's destiny is determined. This is as true with a ministry team as it is with any other team. When you invite people who love God and care for people and who have a vision for the ministry, and you organize them properly, great things can happen.

A useful pattern is the "Reach-Grow-Send" ministry cycle. We want to reach those people whose hearts and gifts we believe will contribute to the work of the team. We then want to grow with them in the discipleship and fellowship of the team and in the use of their gifts in ministry. Finally, we want to send them to serve with some responsibility on behalf of the team. Ultimately, we send them to "Reach-Grow-Send" still others.[1] In this chapter I will look at ways to identify prospective team members and ways to go about inviting them onto the team.

---

1. In a broader sense, the "Reach-Grow-Send" cycle represents basic defining practices for growing disciples. First we "reach" those uncommitted to Jesus Christ and uninvolved in the church, then we "grow" one another as disciples of Jesus Christ, and finally we "send" one another to serve in the church and world. When used to identify and invite new members onto a ministry team, the basic concept of the cycle is the same except that "reach" in this context shifts from a missional focus (the unchurched) to an "involvement" focus (the churched).

Asking God to Raise Up Servants

Jesus told his disciples, "Ask the Lord of the harvest, therefore, to send out workers into his harvest field" (Matt. 9:38). Go and do likewise. Pray that God will raise up people for your ministry team — individuals who love God, who care about people, and who are willing to use their gifts in service of the team's vision. Praying for new team members is part of the team leader's ongoing devotional life, and it is also a corporate spiritual discipline of the team.

One useful method of praying for new team members involves "praying through" a list of all of the people from which new team members may potentially come. If the team's ministry is something like a Bible-study class or a women's group, begin with the list of those involved in the ministry. If the team's ministry involves a task, such as handling the sanctuary sound system or delivering Meals on Wheels, then use the church membership list for your list of prospective new members. If the church is very large, the list may simply be a compilation of all those people whom current team members know.

Have the team pray through the list, one name at a time, asking that God will lead people to join the team or work with the ministry of the team. If the list is long, break it into sections and use one list during each meeting. Praying for people in this way not only enlists God's help in raising up new team members; it also sharpens the team's alertness to people's needs. Few things open our eyes to opportunities for ministry more effectively than praying for people by name.

Finally, before you actually invite someone to join your team, pray for guidance and wisdom. Pray that the prospective team member will respond to your vision and that by God's grace, your invitation will be an encouragement to her. Pray that she will join your team unless there are issues in her life that would prevent her from fully participating or that would suggest there are other and more fruitful places for her to serve.

Identifying Prospective Members

Drawing New Team Members from Several Possible Sources

The vital ministry team remains alert to all of the ways in which God may bring people to join in its work.

When possible, it invites people from the ministry or group it serves to join the team, just as Jesus called the Twelve from his wider group of disciples: "When morning came, he called his disciples to him and chose twelve of them, whom he also designated apostles" (Luke 6:13). If the ministry is a Wednesday-morning Bible class, team members will be drawn from the class. If the ministry involves women of the congregation, team members will come from participants in the women's ministries and from the women in the congregation.

Sometimes people are added to a ministry team by means of an election. Elders, deacons, and others responsible for leading the entire congregation are typically chosen by election. Elections for leadership positions are often common in the organized ministries of traditional congregations such as ministries to men and women. If people must be added to a ministry team by election, lead the nominating committee to seek out people who have the qualities of faith, love, and vision the team needs.

Sometimes the best method of adding new people to a ministry team is via self-selection. People step forward on their own initiative and express interest in joining the team. Scott Stevens led our church's ministry to several hundred teenagers in Pittsburgh. When it was time to recruit members for the student ministry team, he would print up and distribute a list of desired qualities such as faithfulness (a relationship with Jesus Christ and a willingness to grow), availability (a willingness to rearrange one's schedule and eliminate other activities), and teachability (the courage to learn and to step out of a known comfort zone in trusting God). He then would invite any student who was interested in serving on the team to attend an overnight training retreat. At the same time, he would personally invite a number of qualified students and adults to attend the retreat. Following the retreat, each candidate would receive the opportunity to join the ministry team and commit to its covenantal agreements. Using this method,

Scott saw consistently highly motivated people "self-select" onto the team.

Some congregations have a ministry mobilization team. This team works to help every participant in the life of the congregation find a place to serve — within the team itself or within the congregation. Such a team employs a formal spiritual-gift assessment and ministry engagement process to provide a systematic way for congregational members to explore their gifts, interests, and talents for ministry and then to connect them to the appropriate ministry teams or opportunities for service.

Resisting the Pressure to Simply Fill Positions

Sometimes the realities of congregational life put considerable pressure on us to find people to fill open leadership positions. It's great to speak of gift-based teams, but what happens when the coordinator of a youth ministry quits? What happens when the key leader of a stewardship ministry suddenly moves on to other things, and she hasn't led a ministry team or developed apprentices so there are no ready heirs to her leadership position? When a key position opens, we may feel a substantial burden to find a replacement as soon as possible, and thus be tempted to disregard the matter of spiritual gifts and abilities. But this puts the effectiveness of the ministry team at risk.

One of my first experiences in ministry was assuming leadership of a congregation's Sunday School. In the months prior to my involvement, a postcard had been mailed to every Sunday School teacher with this question: "Will you teach Sunday School next year? Yes or No?" It gave those teachers a way out with honor, and twenty teachers took early retirement! I found myself calling the entire congregation, from the Adams to the Zechariahs, asking, "Will you teach Sunday School?" and hearing the common reply, "No." I'll never forget the pressure I felt to "fill positions." When someone finally said they'd handle the "Wee Walker Class," the three-year-olds, I took the rest of the day off to celebrate.

To address the development of leadership in that Sunday School, we organized each class with a teacher ministry team and made the teams responsible to invite new teachers onto the team. We discovered that active church members could make very sound decisions about whom to invite onto their teams, and that certainly made my life much less stressful.

As this example shows, the pressure to "fill slots" diminishes as the congregation or ministry moves increasingly to team-based ministry because ministry teams develop leaders and provide far more consistency in leadership to a ministry. Still, that pressure to fill a vacancy sometimes remains. Remember that just because a person is willing to fill an open position, the search for a suitable person isn't necessarily over. Keep looking for that person who is particularly gifted and keenly interested in taking on the position. But remember too that a willing heart can make all the difference.

Considering Key Issues in Identifying Team Members

When identifying prospective team members, there are many issues to consider, some of them dependent on the nature of the team's ministry. Ask key questions: What kinds of people will best serve the needs of our team in terms of spiritual gifts, abilities, experiences, and interests? Who would be eager to use their gifts and energy to fulfill our team's vision? Teams with a specific task responsibility will be more interested in people with skills related to the work they have to accomplish. Leadership and teaching teams will need people with deep and mature faith as well as those with task-related skills and people skills.

Search Out a Serving Heart

You might think that spiritual giftedness and an interest in a particular ministry are what you most need to look for in a prospective team member. But these things, though very significant, do not constitute the primary reason to invite a person onto a team. Look first for the person with a serving heart. "Each of you should look not only to your own interests, but also to the interests of others. Your attitude should be the same as that of Christ Jesus" (Phil. 2:4-5). Although gifts and interests vary widely among us, a humble, serving spirit is common to all sincere followers of Jesus Christ. And it is interesting to note that it is not unusual for a team to accomplish tasks that require abilities with which no team member is particularly gifted. Suppose the team needs someone to speak publicly on behalf of the team's ministry, and no one feels that they will be able to do it with particular eloquence or comfort? A serving spirit always trumps spiritual gifts. We should remember that when Moses said, "Who am I that I should go to Pharaoh?" God replied, "Go, for I will be with you." Ultimately, it is the God who is with us who ministers through our willing hearts. When people are willing to serve, even if it involves doing something that isn't their "favorite thing," then, by the grace of God, they're going to find a way to accomplish the team's mission.

Related to this idea of the serving heart is the understanding that ministry is a lifestyle to be lived, not merely a spiritual gift to be exercised or a program to be run. Although a team member can learn this after she joins the team, it is wonderful when she grasps this from the beginning. It means she joins the team knowing that Christ, who is in her, has something he wants to do through her, whatever her role on the team may be and wherever she lives her daily life.

Consider a Person's Interests, Spiritual Gifts, and Abilities

Is a prospective team member particularly interested in your team's vision? Interest in ministry combined with a serving spirit is a powerful combination. Even without knowing such a person's particular competencies, you already know the heart is there. Invite him to join your team and figure out how he will serve as his "fit" with the team grows.

It is perfectly appropriate for a team to ask, "What abilities, spiritual gifts, and experience does our team need?" Teams often need people who can fulfill particular responsibilities. It's natural to want a sense of "fit" between the potential teammate and the people on the team and between the potential teammate and the ministry he or she will be asked to do. If you need a person to coordinate the small-group ministry, for example, look for someone with experience and a heart for small groups.

A variety of programs and gift-assessment instruments are com-

mercially available to assist congregations in developing a congregational ministry mobilization team, which I mentioned earlier.[2] It uses
spiritual-gift identification and ministry-interest assessment tools as
well as formal ministry deployment and engagement systems. Such a
mobilization team offers a comprehensive, ongoing means of engaging
every willing church participant in ministry.

People who go through spiritual-gift assessment processes but
don't get connected to a place to serve are a bit like horses milling
around the barnyard. They are able to work, but they need a harness to
join them to a team. That is why a mobilization team combines various
means of assessing a person's spiritual gifts and interests in ministry
with a system for identifying service opportunities in the church and
community. The team links the person to an appropriate assignment
and provides the follow-through to make sure the connection takes
hold.

At times a ministry team will need to identify a person's spiritual
gifts and abilities without having access to these more sophisticated
ministry engagement systems. Some years ago, Ray Stedman brought
great attention to the discovery of spiritual gifts. I have always appreciated the simplicity of his approach to it, which may be summarized
with these simple questions:

1. Do you see the gift in you?
2. Do others see the gift in you?
3. Does using the gift bear fruit?[3]

2. See Sue Mallory's excellent book entitled *The Equipping Church* (Grand Rapids:
Zondervan, 2001), and visit her web site: www.connextion.org. See also Sue Mallory and
Brad Smith, *Equipping Church Guidebook* (Grand Rapids: Zondervan, 2001); Bruce L.
Bugbee, Don Cousins, and Bill Hybels, *Network: Understanding God's Design for You in the
Church* (Grand Rapids: Zondervan, 1994); Wayne Cordeiro, *Doing Church as a Team* (Ventura,
Calif.: Regal Books, 2001); and Rick Warren, *The Purpose Driven Church* (Grand Rapids:
Zondervan, 1995). You can also explore the DESIGN approach of Wayne Cordeiro and the
New Hope Christian Fellowship (www.eNewHope.org), Lifekeys (www.LifeKeys.com), and
the SHAPE ministry of Saddleback Church (www.saddleback.com).

3. Ray Stedman, "Equipped for Community," *HIS Magazine*, March 1972, pp. 2-3, 25-
26. See also his *Body Life* (Ventura, Calif.: Regal Books, 1995). For an excellent discussion
of spiritual gifts and ministry teams, see Brian Kelley Bauknight, *Body Building: Creating
a Ministry Team through Spiritual Gifts* (Nashville: Abingdon Press, 1996).

As a ministry team meets and ministers over an extended period of time, the team members will grow to know one another well and will be increasingly able to offer insight into each other's spiritual gifts and God-given abilities. Think of five people you know well in your church, and you will immediately realize you have some sense of their strengths, gifts, and passion for ministry. When our personal knowledge of people is combined with a more formal gift-discovery procedure, it can be a very perceptive means of helping people discover where they fit.

Finding the right people is key to a team's success and an individual's joy in service — and that includes honoring the way in which someone has used their gifts for many years. "Let's ask Janice to join the worship leadership team," someone might say. "She's been in charge of the sanctuary flowers for years. She'd probably appreciate a change." But Janice's heart is in creating aesthetic beauty, not offering leadership. So she should be honored, appreciated, and respected for her ministry with flowers — and left to enjoy that work.

Consider an Individual's Personal Qualities

The personal qualities of a potential team member are significant insofar as they are relevant to the team's fellowship and ministry. On the one hand, we want to open the door as widely as possible. We don't want to create a list of qualities that are so restrictive that they result in an "in" group and an "out" group, as though joining a ministry team is like getting into a sorority or a fraternity. On the other hand, in order for a team to have a shared life, a new member must be willing to join in and have a heart that lends itself to the vision of the team. Since there are a variety of ministry teams in every congregation, a ministry mobilization team has some flexibility in finding a fit for every person interested in serving.

Look for Faith — A Heart for God

The covenantal agreements of any team will include an emphasis on the spiritual life, and the prospective team member will be asked to practice both corporate and personal spiritual disciplines. A basic openness to growth in discipleship is therefore an essential prerequisite. How can we discern a person's spiritual interests? By listening to what they say and observing the kinds of activities they enjoy in the life of the church. Obviously, only God really knows the true condition of our hearts. When we look for a person with a hunger to grow in God, we make a subjective assessment based on our conversations and observations. Since we are all too aware of our own flaws, we consider someone we might invite onto the team in a spirit of utter humility. We look for someone who humbly seeks to live in a manner worthy of the Lord, fully aware of the reality of his own sin and constant need for grace.

We seek someone who evidences a basic desire to grow in discipleship since we covenant as a team to grow together in Christ. This person may be "young in the faith," may have made a comparatively recent profession of faith. She may not even have a clear idea of her spiritual giftedness yet. But as we hear of her interest in God and observe her willingness to learn and her eagerness to serve, we invite her to join our team. In all humility we rely upon God to help us discern whom he has put into our midst to invite, and when we do invite a person, we entrust both ourselves and that person to God.

What happens if a prospective member on the team isn't spiritually seasoned but is eager to jump in and handle a specific task? Eagerness is a wonderful asset in ministry. If your team requires a level of spiritual maturity, you can challenge this person to function in "the next ring out" — those who serve in the ministry but who aren't on the ministry team itself — by offering him an assignment in which he may employ his energy. If your team is "seeker-sensitive" and is open to the person whose faith is minimally formed, it is perfectly appropriate to invite the person whose faith is new as long as he is willing to participate in the corporate spiritual disciplines of the team. The seeker-sensitive team will modify those disciplines so that they won't intimidate the seeker but will still create fellowship. As the seeker-sensitive team engages in a seeker-appropriate experience of "Word-Share-Prayer," the new member will grow.

Look for Hope — A Heart and a Passion for the Task

Is the prospective team member interested in or open to your ministry's vision? You may invite someone onto your team who really doesn't grasp, at first, what you're doing. A person may join a hospital visitation team or a teaching team or a cooking team out of a willingness to serve but with little understanding of what is really involved. Look for someone who is open to discovering exactly what the team's ministry is and experimenting with her role on the team. Train her. Support her. Remember that vision for ministry is often "more caught than taught." If the team's ministry turns out to be the new member's passion — wonderful. But if it doesn't, then send her with blessing and honor to a different ministry opportunity.

Look for Love — A Heart for People

The prospective team member with a loving heart will automatically want to contribute to the team's own experience of fellowship. If the team's ministry vision involves working directly with people, such as a youth group or a women's group, then some team members with a heart for people are essential. Such a team is best served when it has several people who are willing to minister to individuals on an interpersonal basis as well as several people who are more task-oriented.

I find Chuck Miller's expression "people eyes" an excellent way to help communicate a vision for loving and nurturing people. Those with "people eyes" see people through the eyes of Jesus Christ, see them as people with needs to be met — spiritual, physical, emotional, social, and relational — and look for ways to do so.

Often a new person trying to enter a group feels that the group isn't warm, isn't hospitable, and has no place for them. The group may feel quite warm and hospitable from the inside, but that's because people on the inside are often "people-blind." Those with "people eyes" have a heart for people, have the capacity to focus on one in the midst of many. They are shepherd-minded. Those with "people eyes" see the hurting and comfort them, see those willing to grow spiritually and seek to connect them to God. The Apostle Paul described Timothy as having "people eyes": "I have no one else like him, who takes a genuine interest in your welfare. For everyone looks out for his own interests, not those of Jesus Christ" (Phil. 2:20-21).

Team members with "people eyes" will always keep interpersonal ministry issues on the same plane as program issues. They will ensure that the program is attending to the real needs of those the team serves.

Look for a Willingness to Learn

Another important quality for a prospective member is a willingness to learn, an openness to new ideas, no matter what her level of experience. The people who lead the short-term mission teams in the congregation I serve have considerable experience. Yet they still attend an annual national conference every year just to pick up fresh approaches and ways to improve.

A team that seeks new members who are open to new ideas is going to be a teachable team. It isn't going to be locked into just one way of doing things and will enjoy the process of getting better with new ideas.

Look for Faithfulness and Humility

A priceless quality in a prospective member is faithfulness. Is this person reliable? Does she follow through, do what she says she'll do? Faithfulness is indispensable in team life. It enriches every aspect of it.

Does this person have a humble spirit? Avoid the potential team member who has to be the center of attention, make all the decisions, and dominate the conversation and the action. Instead, look for someone of strength and vision who knows how to be "one among many." Humility goes a long way in team life.

Look for Availability

Availability is not one of the more significant issues that we've been reviewing here — and yet it's extremely important. If, upon inviting a prospective member who is qualified in all other respects, you discover that she cannot meet when the team meets, you might consider changing the team's meeting time, particularly if the team is small.

Personal schedules are always changing and frequently very complex. You may find yourself constantly having to choose between two people whose schedules conflict. No matter when the team meets, there will be some people whose schedule will not permit them to attend. Trust God to lead those individuals to you who can work the team meetings into their schedules.

Concluding Thoughts

It's easy to develop a long list of qualifications for prospective team members, but it's best to keep the list relatively short. Pray for God's guidance, and after humble reflection invite people onto the team who you believe will best serve the ministry and who in turn will be best encouraged by the team.

I remember once hearing Howard Hendricks say that Jesus did not recruit people on the basis of what they were but on the basis of what they would become with him. All you have to do is think of the Apostle Peter — or your own life — to realize the truth of that. So, in team-member recruitment, look for the things we've discussed here, but also see people in terms of growth and development, in terms of what they can become. Reach out to them, then grow with them, and as they are equipped in the practice of ministry, send them to serve within the ministry of the team.

Inviting the Prospective Team Member onto the Team

As I've pointed out, adding a new team member isn't just a matter of filling a position. We know that God is offering service and growth opportunities through us whenever we invite another onto the team. When a person is "called" to a particular ministry (any ministry, whether as church member or pastor), that call is experienced as both an "inner" and an "outer" call. The inner call is the God-given interest, the passion that a person has for a particular area of service, and the outer call is the invitation from the body of believers to engage in that service. When the outer call is confirmed by the inner call, or vice versa, the person understands that God is offering an opportunity to serve. As a result, when we invite a person to join a ministry team, we do so in a spirit of deep humility, knowing that we are the instruments through which God may call a person into specific service. A great many lives may be affected by the answer the person gives.

It's important to make the invitation personal. Jesus didn't say, "Please join my group of twelve!" He said, "Follow me." Invite people to join you as well as the team effort. The invitation isn't just to accomplish a task; it is first of all to become part of a band of brothers and sisters in Christ committed to one another in personal relationship.

When I was serving the Covenant Presbyterian Church near Purdue University, a Purdue student by the name of Steve Ebling began to attend our college ministry. His desire to love God, his heart for people, his kindred spirit, and his cheerful willingness to assume responsibility was obvious to everyone. I took John Stewart, another team member, with me, and we went to visit Steve. I said something like, "Steve, we've enjoyed getting to know you in CCF [College and Career Fellowship]. We've sensed your warm love for Jesus Christ, and we've seen your heart for people and for ministry. On behalf of the central ministry team of CCF, we ask you to pray about committing yourself to us. We will commit ourselves to you, and in turn we will serve the wider CCF ministry, which serves several hundred people. We meet Wednesdays at 6:00 P.M. as a team, for a time of small-group Bible study and prayer. We then lead the large group gathering of CCF that begins at 7:30 P.M. You're clearly gifted as a teacher, and we would like to rely on you to help with teaching the large-group Bible studies on Wednesday nights. Please take two or three days to pray about it, and we'll get back to you to see what your thinking is and find out if you have any additional questions." As you might imagine, Steve joined the team. After graduating from Purdue, he joined the staff of our congregation for a year to lead the entire college ministry before he went to seminary and then on to a wonderful pastoral ministry. It is interesting to realize that Steve's first real ministry training took place on that ministry team, long before he attended seminary.

Asking someone to join your team will require adjustments in her life as well as adjustments in the team's life. Finding the right person in terms of gifts, interest, and attitudes is crucial for the team's ultimate effectiveness. Finding the right place of service so that the individual can make it work in her life is also important. Now, on the one hand, we as followers of Jesus Christ do not understand ourselves as "volunteers," as though faithful obedience to Christ and ministry on his behalf were optional. On the other hand, when a person consents to invest a part of her life in a particular area of service, of course she is a volunteer.

When inviting a person onto a team, be completely honest about what will be required. Give him the list of the team's covenantal agreements (the Seven Threads of Ministry-Team Relationships) and a checklist or summary of the assignment you are giving him. Thoroughly and clearly explain the kind of commitment, time, and work that will be required so that he can make a fully informed decision.

Don't be afraid to ask for a significant commitment. God's people will rise to a challenge. Consider this step-by-step process of inviting a person onto the team.

Get Face to Face

I have often imagined what Barnabas might have said to Saul when Barnabas took the time to travel from Antioch to Tarsus to invite Saul to join the leadership team of the thriving church in Antioch. Whatever he said, it stands as one of the single most significant acts of enlistment in the history of the Christian church — indeed, in all of human history.

Follow the example set by Barnabas. You may prefer to use the phone or e-mail to issue an invitation to a person you know well, but remember that in most instances the greatest invitational impact is made in a face-to-face meeting. When you are together, you can look the person in the eye, invite her to be with you, respond to verbal and non-verbal questions and uncertainties, and pray with her. When you invite a person onto a team this way, you show by example that the team is committed to face-to-face relationships, direct communication, and mutual encouragement.

Use the "With Me" Principle

When you call on the person, take another member of the ministry team with you. This is the "with me" principle in action. Recall that Jesus constantly sent his disciples to accomplish various missions in pairs. Think of Ruth and Naomi, Elijah and Elisha, Mary and Elizabeth, Paul and Barnabas, Paul and Silas, Barnabas and John Mark, the two disciples whom Jesus met on the road to Emmaus. "Two are better than one," we read in Ecclesiastes, "because they have a good return for their work" (4:9).

When you take someone with you, pray together before, during, and after the appointment. And bear in mind the advantages of having a partner. You can show your partner how to invite a person onto the ministry team. The person you are inviting will have someone else who can answer questions and help them get a feeling for the ministry opportunity. And you can grow as friends with your teammate.

Explain the Team Vision

Tell the prospective team member about your vision as a ministry.

> "Our vision is to invite children to faith in Jesus Christ, to equip them as followers of Christ and to send them to ministry."
>
> "Our vision is to involve five hundred men in small groups that meet weekly."
>
> "Our vision is to provide outstanding audio in the church sanctuary."
>
> "Our vision is to develop disciples through the mothers of preschoolers ministry."

Explain your vision, its ramifications, and the consequences of fulfilling it. Review the present level of the team's accomplishment of its vision. Cover both the problems you are encountering and the possibilities that you see. Share your vision with enthusiasm; give the person something to be passionate about.

Review the Team Covenant

The formal expression of the team's covenantal agreements (detailed in Chapter Seven) provides a benchmark for the quality of team life and team members' interpersonal relationships. Take a copy of these agreements to give to the prospective team member. Review these covenantal agreements with him, and when he joins the team, review them with the entire team again as a means of reinforcing them and reminding the team of its commitment to practice Christian fellowship and to serve with excellence.

Explain the Ministry Description

Explain clearly what your team will expect this prospective team member to do, the tasks, deadlines, and other people she will work with. This is best accomplished with a written ministry description that explains things clearly and succinctly. Remember that no one likes hearing the words, "Oh, by the way . . ." after saying yes to a project. Provide as complete an understanding of what will be required as you can.

Explain what you see in the prospective candidate that has led you to invite her to join your team, or why the ministry mobilization team thinks she would be a good match with your team. Tell her that as you get to know each other more deeply on the team, there may be shifts in responsibilities to better tap into one another's abilities, available time, and willingness to serve. It's true that the prospective member wants to join the team because of its vision, but she will stay on the team because she experiences the team's heart, its fellowship. In that ongoing fellowship, task assignments will be adjusted according to the needs of the present situation.

Occasionally you may invite a person onto your team who has a heart for God and for people and who shares the ministry vision of the team without knowing what her particular role is going to be from the outset. The team will match her gifts, interests, and willingness to serve with its ministry needs. If you eventually discover her best "fit" would be with a different ministry or team, then bless her and send her to the place of more effective service.

Discuss the Length of Service

Establish the basic length of service you are asking for — typically one, two, or three years. Remember, though, that God has gifted people with the abilities and passion for particular ministries, and when they serve in those ministries for extended periods of time, some real expertise and impact can develop. For that reason, it is wise to have a way to allow people to extend their service as long as they have a passion for the vision and an effective involvement on the team. Say to the prospective member, "You may serve on this team as long as you have heart and vision for the ministry."

In the congregation that I am serving, Keith and Darlene Bachman, Darren and Lori Bowers, Tim and Rose Comer, Deac Dressing, Beth Lamb, Joe and Margie Veltri, and Bob and Sandy Weiss have served on the youth ministry's central ministry team for over ten years. Their love for teenagers and their grasp of the dynamics of youth ministry is at the highest level, strengths no one can develop in a two-year stint as a "youth advisor."

Also let the prospective member know that when he believes God is leading him to something else, he can be sent elsewhere with the team's blessing. Bear in mind that there is a vast difference between leaving and being sent. To *leave* means literally "to no longer be a part of." To leave is to go with no implication of honor, blessing, or love. To be *sent*, on the other hand, is to go with blessing, to go to minister on behalf of the team in some new setting. The formal connection to the team may end, but genuine friendships that grew during team life will continue with blessing and love.

Give the Person Time to Decide

Ask the prospective member to take time to pray about the invitation, to discuss it with family and friends, and to think it through. If a person joins a team feeling some pressure from the one who invited him, it will often happen that his level of commitment and service to the team will be less than anticipated. Remember my earlier story of inviting Steve Ebling onto the CCF ministry team. Say to this person, "Please take two or three days to pray about this invitation, and we'll get back to you to see what your thinking is. If you have any additional questions, let us know." Then be sure to make a follow-up call in a couple of days. If you wait any longer, this person may find your request supplanted by new demands and opportunities that have come his way in the meantime.

If the prospective member says "Yes," then celebrate with him. If he says "No, thank you," be sure he knows that your appreciation for him remains at a high level, and that you look forward to continuing fellowship with him in the life of the congregation.

Conclusion

Identifying and inviting ministry-team members can be challenging, but it is also very significant and rewarding work. When you invite people who love the Lord and who embrace the vision of your ministry, wonderful things can and do happen. Remember to always ask the Lord for guidance, recalling the counsel of James: "If any of you is lacking in wisdom, ask God, who gives to all generously and ungrudgingly, and it will be given you" (1:5, NRSV).

Nurturing Ministry-Team Life

I loved watching my son, Lee, run in his high-school track meets. Lee would get set at the starting line by adjusting his feet on the starting blocks. When the gun sounded, I could see his ankles, knees, and hips all working together in triple extension for maximum power. Traditional committees are often geared to address a particular task; rarely do they develop the discipleship and fellowship of their members or address the specific needs of the people involved in the committee's task. Such an experience is transformed with the addition of the "triple extension movement" of ministry-team life that begins with growth in discipleship and vibrant fellowship and then flows decisively outward in the accomplishment of ministry or missional vision.

In Chapter Seven I discuss the kind of ministry-team fellowship that develops disciples of its members and nurtures quality friendships among them. This involves specific patterns of team life, such as the small-group experience and prayer partnerships. It also involves the establishment of the covenantal agreements known as the Seven Threads of Ministry-Team Relationships.

In Chapter Eight I explain the defining visions of a disciple-growing ministry that may be employed to grow disciples both among the team members and among the people to whom the team is in ministry.

In Chapters Nine and Ten I explore the nature of the team's double focus of ministry on people and program. The team handles planning, program, and the deployment of personnel much as any task-oriented committee or board would. But the team's involvement with people potentially goes far beyond a typical committee "batch processing" approach by encouraging the direct interpersonal ministry of team members with those whom their team serves.

CHAPTER SEVEN

Building Ministry-Team Life

Years ago I remember reading the story of John R. Mott, who became a great leader of Christian ministry early in the twentieth century. At one point Mott describes his interview with George Williams, the founder of the YMCA. "As that never-to-be-forgotten hour drew toward a close, I ventured to ask this question: 'Mr. Williams, what was in your mind and in the minds of your colleagues which led you to form the first Young Men's Christian Association?' Quickly he replied, 'We had only one thing in mind and that was to bind our little company together in order that we might the better lead our comrades to Christ, and in order that we might share with one another our personal experiences of Christ.'"[1]

Although Williams didn't use the language of "team," he and his friends clearly served on a ministry team with three essential movements: growth in discipleship ("to share our experiences of Christ"), growth in fellowship ("to bind our little company together") and growth in ministry ("in order to lead our comrades to Christ"). These three functions are, of course, the triple extension movement of the ministry team: discipleship, fellowship, and ministry. In this chapter we consider the elements of a fellowship that grows disciples and deploys itself in ministry.

---

1. John R. Mott, *Confronting Young Men with the Living Christ* (New York: Association Press, 1923), p. 14.

Practicing the Spiritual Disciplines
of Discipleship and Fellowship

Fellowship means so much more than just a group of Christians gathered in the same room. Fellowship is relational, involving deep, trusting relationships with one another and our Lord. We read about it in the book of First John: "We proclaim to you what we have seen and heard, so that you also may have fellowship [*koinonia*] with us. And our fellowship is with the Father and with his Son, Jesus Christ" (1:3). *Koinonia* experiences Jesus Christ as its center and its organizing purpose. Today all sorts of team-building exercises and activities are widely used to develop camaraderie, cohesion, and mutual trust: from tackling rope courses, to taking the Myers-Briggs test, to engaging in an assortment of affirmation exercises. Although these and many other activities can be highly effective in producing common bonds among team members, ministry teams need some regular patterns of activity that will root their relationships in Jesus Christ and connect them to one another.

Ministry-team fellowship doesn't automatically happen. Committees and other ministry organizations are often made up of highly motivated people who carry out an assignment together and then go back to their individual lives with little ongoing interaction. But, using the patterns of Jesus' ministry, we will see how the elements of Bible study, prayer, shared meals, and annual retreats may be structured into the lifestyle of virtually any ministry team. It is also possible to add these elements to existing committees and other ministry groups to move them toward a more complete ministry-team experience.

Enjoying Small-Group Life

Small groups are one of the fastest-growing changes in the design of church programming today.[2] For many believers, the small group is the

---

2. For a detailed discussion of the small group, see my book entitled *Small Group Life*, available from www.vitalfaithresources.com or Vital Faith Resources, P.O. Box 18378, Pittsburgh, PA 15236.

only context in which they experience face-to-face fellowship, getting to know others well, and just being loved. Small-group life is integral and essential to ministry-team life: it is the primary means by which team members grow in Christian fellowship. Such groups are also among the most effective means of fostering growth in discipleship. Thus the small-group experience of a ministry team simultaneously accomplishes two of the basic movements of ministry-team life: discipleship and fellowship. In fact, one of the simplest and most complete ways to describe a ministry team is as the marriage of small-group life and committee function. Well-equipped team leaders who understand and embrace small-group life are essential to the development of team-based ministry in a congregation.[3]

For a number of years I belonged to a committee that was responsible for bringing speakers into our city who could introduce pastors and church members to state-of-the-art instruction in the dynamics of church vitality. We were a diverse bunch, representing inner-city and suburban congregations, large and small congregations, with white and black members. Our committee met for only two hours a month, and like most such experiences, the meeting was mainly an interruption in our usual routines that found us getting together with people we hardly knew. Some of us did it because we believed in the vision. Some of us did it because it was an assignment given to us. We met to plan the programs and divide up the work to be done, and then we headed home.

After a year of meeting like this, we decided to begin our meetings by setting our committee work aside and spending our first thirty min-

---

3. Some tremendous resources are available to support the small-group life of your ministry teams and indeed of your congregation as a whole. An excellent resource for growing community through the small group is Richard C. Meyer's *One Anothering*, a three-volume series on small-group life. For a thorough study of the biblical and historical foundations for small groups, see Gareth Icenogle, *Biblical Foundations for Small Group Ministry* (Downers Grove, Ill.: InterVarsity Press, 1994). See also Thomas G. Bandy, *Christian Chaos* (Nashville: Abingdon Press, 1999); E. Stanley Ott, *Small Group Life*; Carl F. George with Warren Bird, *Nine Keys to Effective Small Group Leadership* (Mansfield, Ohio: Kingdom Publishing, 1997); Bill Donahue, *Leading Life-Changing Small Groups* (Grand Rapids: Zondervan, 1996); and Paul Borthwick et al., *Small Group Ministry* (Loveland, Colo.: Vital Ministry Books, 1999).

utes together in a small-group format. (We determined to work more efficiently in the remaining time to keep from increasing the length of the meetings.) So we engaged in the "Word-Share-Prayer" pattern. We spent ten minutes engaging in substantive conversation about a brief passage of Scripture, fifteen minutes sharing the blessings and concerns of our lives with each other, and five minutes praying for one another by name.

It seemed like such a simple change, but over the course of a year, a marvelous thing began to happen. Genuine friendship began to grow among us. Charles Ham, the pastor of an inner-city church in a distressed neighborhood, began bringing his infant daughter along. She charmed us as we worked. Soon Charles and I started to meet for lunch just to share what was in our our hearts. When Charles died of sudden heart failure, we all mourned his death. All of us also delighted in the perspective brought by Alan Trafford, who came to our city from England. I enjoyed visiting him at home and sharing in a wonderful English meal cooked by his wife, Lesley, and meeting their two sons. As a group we all rejoiced and commiserated together about the ups and downs of our teenagers. In short, instead of remaining a committee of people who were at best acquaintances sharing a common task, we became a ministry team experiencing fellowship rooted in our Lord.

Small groups grow depth in discipleship *and* fellowship precisely because they are small, because people are face to face, because no one can be anonymous, because they are centered in Bible study and prayer. Small groups may have as few as two or three people and as many as fourteen. "For where two or three come together in my name, there am I with them" (Matt. 18:20). Once a group exceeds fourteen people, the depth of sharing decreases. For this reason, an effective ministry team that grows larger than that finds ways to form subgroups within the overall team so that people continue to share on a face-to-face basis.

During the time your team participates in small-group life, immerse yourselves in studying Scripture, sharing your personal lives, and praying for one another. This "Word-Share-Prayer" pattern is pictured on the following page as the Discipleship Triangle.

As the triangle illustrates, team members engage in an interactive experience in which they focus on Scripture, Christian faith, their personal lives, ways of encouraging one another, and prayer. Although

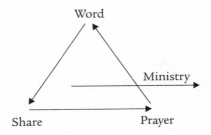

The Discipleship Triangle
(This originally appeared in my book *Small Group Life*)

matters of common ministry concern may arise, the team should keep the focus on simply "being" the people of God, enjoying fellowship with one another and the Lord. Ministry, as the Discipleship Triangle indicates, flows out of the team's experience of fellowship and discipleship.

Ideally the team should use an approach to Bible study that guides them in conversation about a biblical text. Team members may open their Bibles to a particular passage or use a Bible study guidebook. In the congregation I serve, we have discovered one particularly useful tool is the one-page "Guided Bible Study" format that directs team members to read a biblical text, reflect on it, respond to it, and jot down any prayer requests they may have. Guided Bible Studies are easy to develop and are quite useful in drawing people into Scripture.[4]

A ministry team usually begins its regular meetings with small-group life. If the team takes the first thirty minutes of a one-and-a-half to two-hour meeting for its small-group life, then the total time for the Bible-study portion will generally be ten to fifteen minutes. This is not an "in-depth" study, but it lets the team focus on one or two key ideas. Sometimes a ministry team will meet at different times during the week for small-group sessions to devote more time to Bible study.

When the ministry team meets and the initial "hello's" have been exchanged, the team is ready to begin the "Word" portion of its time.

4. These are described more fully in Appendix Three, which illustrates the Guided Bible Study format and lists a number of short biblical passages that you may find useful for your team's Bible study.

At my church we have found it a useful practice to allow five minutes for team members to study the selected text in silence. This allows everyone to engage the biblical text and to be engaged by it, without distracting conversation. Then insights can be shared during the remaining Bible-study time. The team leader or the Bible-study leader may wish to bring this study to a close with a very short "teaching" for the team based on the chosen text.

At the appropriate time, the team leader or a designated time-keeper gently but firmly moves the team from Bible study to the sharing of lives. Team members take the next ten minutes to share recent experiences, both blessings and concerns. Since a small group of ten people could easily take forty-five minutes to do this, members should touch only on things of greatest interest or concern to them. If someone is facing tremendous difficulty, the team obviously needs to take the time to minister to that person.

Finally, take five minutes to pray for one another by name, including those who are absent. Then begin the rest of your work as a ministry team, your ministry now flowing out of your fellowship.

Remember that it is perfectly appropriate to schedule longer times of "Word-Share-Prayer" to allow more opportunity to encourage one another in your walk with Christ. And there are many possible variations of this meeting format.[5] My wife, Ann Marie, began a ministry to women in the marketplace by calling a team of similar heart to join her. The team begins by taking some time for Bible study, next processes the details of its ministry plans, and then spends an hour or two sharing, laughing, and praying together. They often go home late and happy, having taken extended time out of their very busy lives to really enter into one another's worlds.

Small-group life thrives in direct relation to the time the group spends together. Weekly meetings are ideal because they permit a vigorous continuity of relationship to develop among the members. Groups that meet less frequently can still experience meaningful fellowship if they follow the general rule that the longer the time between meetings, the longer the meetings themselves need to be. The intensity of team fellowship and the effectiveness and scope of its ministry are also di-

---

5. See Appendix Two for some helpful specifics about team-meeting formats.

rectly related to time spent together. Ministry teams that meet every week experience the deepest fellowship and accomplish the greatest scope of ministry.

Under the monthly committee system, a person could participate in several different activities at once without too many time commitments. When ministry teams meet as frequently as once a week or twice a month, most team members will limit their congregational involvement to one or two ministry teams (in addition to corporate worship and other occasional activities). A person on a ministry team may in turn lead or be a part of an affiliate ministry team. To develop real relationships with the people on two teams and to carry out the responsibilities for each team can take up all of the time for church-based ministry that the average participant is able to give. As a result, the shift to team-based leadership in a congregation will mean that most people will be involved in fewer ministries, but the impact of those teams on the participant's experience of fellowship will be greater.

One final note: Plan to begin your ministry-team meetings with the small-group experience, not end with it. Once members begin to talk about matters of task and program and discuss who's going to do what, they will find it difficult to shift the conversation to Bible study, sharing, and prayer. Task details have a way of multiplying, and once they enter the conversation, there will be no end of them. So be the people of God *before* you do the work of the people of God.

Establishing Prayer Partnerships

Prayer partnerships are a terrific means of helping team members grow in discipleship and friendship. The beauty of prayer partnerships is that they make our general commitment "to pray for one another" specific and personal. On a recent trip to Malawi, I had the pleasure of entering into a number of prayer partnerships with the Christians of that country. When I think of Malawi now, it is people who come to mind: Elivey Chirwa, Daniel Gunya, Mathias Hauya, William Katunga, Paul and Doreen Mtali, Silas and Margaret Ncozana, Bernard Thomas, and others. Our prayer partnerships have made our fellowship deeply personal.

To form prayer partnerships, organize your ministry team into groups of two or three. The members of each prayer duo or trio agree to pray for one another daily. They may also agree to a phone conversation or an e-mail communication once a week to share answered prayer or make new prayer requests. Rotate partners once a month, so that team members may learn to love and pray for everyone on the team. God has a way of giving us heart for those for whom we pray.

When the prayer partners are willing, they may go beyond praying *for* one another daily and begin praying *with* one another weekly. Whether in person or by phone, they share the blessings and concerns of their lives with one another and then, in a conversational style, pray for one another.

One way to give every prayer partnership some basic prayers to use is to suggest drawing on the prayers in the Bible, such as Ephesians 1:15-19; Colossians 1:9-12; and a number of the psalms, such as Psalm 100. The partners simply substitute their names for those in the Bible's prayer and pray it for each other. Here is an example that employs Ephesians 3:16-19:

> I pray that out of God's glorious riches he may strengthen *Marty and me* with power through his Spirit in *our* inner being, so that Christ may dwell in *our* hearts through faith. And I pray that *Marty and I,* being rooted and established in love, may have power, together with all the saints, to grasp how wide and long and high and deep is the love of Christ, and to know this love that surpasses knowledge — that *we* may be filled to the measure of all the fullness of God.

Sharing Meals Together

Dick Halverson, former chaplain of the U.S. Senate, used to say there was something sacramental about Christians eating a meal together. He wasn't saying that the shared meal held the same meaning as Holy Communion. Yet I see his point. When we join with others who acknowledge the Lord's presence and share a common meal, there is a special quality and depth to our fellowship. That Jesus regularly broke bread in fellowship reminds us of his real presence whenever we share a meal with other believers. Indeed, after his resurrection, Jesus revealed himself to the two disciples at Emmaus when they broke bread together.

Similarly, we may enjoy a special depth of fellowship and friendship that comes only when we eat with one another. So make sharing meals a regular practice of your ministry team. The meals may be as simple or as elaborate as you want to make them. Think again of the early church as described in Acts: "They broke bread in their homes and ate together with glad and sincere hearts" (2:46). Eating together in smaller groups was essential to their experience of fellowship, and it is key to our experience of fellowship as well.

If you are too busy to schedule meals in addition to your meetings, then plan to carry out your regular meeting agenda while you eat together. It is perfectly appropriate to enjoy each other's company over a meal for a while and then attend to the regular agenda of the team. Meet in a home where a simple meal has been prepared, or meet in the back corner of a restaurant. Or bring sack lunches or fast food to your regular meeting place. If the team has very busy people, pick up some coldcuts at a deli or have a pizza delivered. Remember that what you eat and where you eat are not nearly as significant as that you eat together. The food is not the point. It is only a means to the end of fellowship.

Some teams will find the sharing of meals built into their ministry. A Habitat for Humanity team, for example, or a short-term mission team will automatically share meals during their workdays. However, many teams will share meals together only when they are scheduled intentionally. So make breaking bread together a matter of team discipline. One way to do this is to determine when you will eat together over the course of a year, so that sharing meals is not a matter of whim but a scheduled facet of your life together.

When you begin a meal, acknowledge the Lord's presence with you in the prayer of Grace. Then relax and enjoy one another's company. Spend some time in general conversation, sharing news about recent events in your lives. You may then move on to the ministry issues that your team needs to resolve. Set a minimum number of times that the team will eat together during the year — say, four times: fall, winter, spring, and summer. Then do it!

Going on a Retreat

In addition to sharing meals, there are many other activities that can build the spirit and depth of the team's fellowship. In her book entitled *Turning Committees into Communities*, Roberta Hestenes argues persuasively for an annual retreat lasting at least Friday night through Saturday.[6] As a way to really develop relationships and do some thorough reflection on the team's ministry, the retreat is without parallel. Recall that Jesus frequently took his disciples on retreats. Clearly he considered this "getaway time" essential for the growth of fellowship. Remember, too, that retreats lend themselves to laughter and fun, which invigorate the spirit of a healthy team.

Other fellowship-building experiences can be as simple as going to a movie, to a ballgame, to a restaurant, to a fireworks display — anything that team members enjoy doing together. It's just a matter of deciding to do it and doing it often enough to enjoy one another's company, but not so often that it becomes a scheduling headache for everyone. Special events shared just once or twice a year can be tremendously encouraging. Again, put this on your calendar!

These special times provide a great opportunity to include other family members in Christian fellowship. Spouses and parents of team members will find they are welcome in the group. And children love it. They learn to see their parents' ministry team as a genuine experience of what Christian fellowship is all about. The ministry team becomes a group that they feel a part of, too. And remember that you'll be far more capable of loving and encouraging others on your team when you know and come to love their families as well.

Concluding Thoughts

Obviously, the meeting frequency and nature of some teams lend themselves easily to the introduction of small-group life, prayer partnerships, shared meals, annual retreats, and other means of developing team fel-

---

6. Roberta Hestenes, *Turning Committees into Communities* (Colorado Springs: NavPress, 1991), pp. 24-26.

lowship. Other teams may find it requires more creativity to reshape team life with some or all of these practices. But doing that extra work is well worth it, since these practices are what allow teams to develop the kind of fellowship that will enrich and sustain them.

Practicing Covenant-Based Fellowship: Employing the Seven Threads of Ministry-Team Relationships

Mike Krzyzewski, basketball coach at Duke University, offers some wise comments about teams. "When you first assemble a group," he says, "it's not a team right off the bat. It is a collection of individuals, just like any other group. And there is some truth to the adage 'You're only as good as your talent.' As a matter of fact, I think everyone understands that you can't win championships without talent. So assembling skillful individuals as part of your team is a given. Then, of course, it becomes a matter of motivating those people to perform as a team."[7] Team life is about the experience of individual hearts joining to become a "team heart." Team heart is team chemistry, the relationships among members creating the experience of fellowship. Of course, experiencing team heart is not automatic; not everyone fits in easily. Sometimes an individual's particular approach to life or quirk of personality may make him or her a challenge for other team members to identify with. But the team does its best to take people with a great variety of personalities and interests and forge them into a unified whole.

All healthy groups have basic guidelines or covenantal agreements for conduct that the members of the group accept and adhere to. Team heart grows out of the faithful following of these guidelines, which express basic courtesies and commitments. A healthy team identifies key covenants for their life together — enough to give shape to their experience of fellowship, but not so many that they become an oppressive list of do's and don'ts.[8]

7. Mike Krzyzewski with Donald T. Phillips, *Leading with the Heart* (New York: Warner Books, 2000), p. 22.

8. George Cladis offers some excellent guidelines for the development of a team covenant in his book entitled *Leading the Team-Based Church*. He writes about obtaining team-leader commitment to the covenant; about allowing sufficient time for the team

Any piece of cloth is simply many threads woven together into a single fabric. Similarly, the fellowship experienced by a team is made up of many personal relationships woven into a whole. That wholeness comes about when the team engages in and honors certain covenantal agreements — what I call the "seven threads" of healthy ministry-team relationships. Let's examine them more closely here.

Thread One   *Spiritual Disciplines: We Engage*
                  in the Disciplines of the Christian Faith

Our earnest desire is to grow in loving, faithful relationship with our Lord, experiencing his grace and love and offering that grace and love to others. Out of love for our Lord, we commit ourselves wholeheartedly to the disciplines of the Christian faith. We know that these spiritual disciplines do not in themselves earn God's grace, but are means by which that grace may grow in our lives and extend through us to others. We know that our salvation is by faith, believing in Jesus Christ alone, and that by means of these disciplines we are both serving and pleasing Christ and showing gratitude for the grace God has given us.

We covenant as a ministry team to practice the corporate spiritual disciplines of small-group life: studying the Bible together, sharing our lives with one another, and praying for one another. We engage in formal prayer partnerships. We break bread with one another, sharing in hospitality and in friendship. We commit ourselves to attend corporate worship and to build the quality of the fellowship of both congregation and ministry team as we practice humility and mutual service.

We covenant to engage in personal spiritual disciplines such as regularly reading the Bible, praying in daily devotions, and worshipping with a congregation. We lovingly encourage one another in the practice of these personal spiritual disciplines. And we covenant to pray for our ministry team as a whole and for each member on the team.

---

to develop a covenant that reflects their hearts, which involves honesty and self-disclosure; and about acknowledging sin and recognizing our need for confession, vulnerability, and grace. Cladis suggests that covenants should be specific without containing minutiae and that they should be reviewed often and revised when appropriate. See *Leading the Team-Based Church* (San Francisco: Jossey-Bass, 1999), pp. 41-45.

Thread Two   Face-to-Face Relationships: We Develop
Friendships with Other Team Members

We covenant to build real face-to-face friendships that make personal relationships a higher priority than even our team's ministry. In the context of true relationship, we are free to shape our common vision and share ideas with each other. We respect one another, love one another, and serve one another. In face-to-face relationships, everything is kept "on the table," without hidden agendas or concerns. We tell one another what we think, and we move ahead together.

We practice hospitality with one another, welcoming each other into our lives and spending time together for the primary purpose of growing in friendship, not just to accomplish a task. We practice reconciliation when discord surfaces among us. We agree to disagree fairly and respectfully, and to model love, dignity, and unity to the congregation or wider ministry. We adhere to the "Good Report Principle."[9] When we speak about others, we speak well of them, treating them with great respect out of respect for our Lord, even if we don't always agree with them.

Thread Three   Confidentiality: We Respect the
Confidences of Others

We covenant to keep one another's confidences. Confidentiality involves trust, and when we trust one another within the team, we grow in unity and heart. Personal information that we share with one another stops with us unless we have permission to pass it on. Concerns shared within the team as matters for prayer, personal support, and encouragement are to be kept among team members even after the team disbands or certain members leave the team. We do not ask others on the team to betray confidences in order to advance our ministry.

Confidentiality simply means that we respect one another enough to trust each other with what we say. When we experience an atmo-

9. This is a phrase used by Ron Rand, the president of UpBuilding Ministries in Cincinnati, Ohio.

sphere of affirmation and confidentiality, we are free to be vulnerable and to speak of the deeper concerns of our hearts. At the same time, we will act decisively if we learn that a life is in danger — that a person is considering suicide or is being physically or sexually abused. To ignore such situations would represent the very opposite of Christian fellowship.

Thread Four   *Communication: We Communicate*
                         Directly and Thoroughly

We covenant to communicate constantly, and we try to communicate person-to-person whenever possible. For routine matters, using written notes, e-mail, or voice mail is fine, but we don't initiate conversation about issues of significance this way. Significant issues are those that "grab us in the gut." They may involve a major assignment, a difficult undertaking, or a confrontation.

Being committed to face-to-face relationships means we do not communicate through a third party. Another way of saying this is we do not make bank shots. In the game of pool, one way to knock a ball into the pocket is by banking the ball off the side rail and into the pocket. In human relationships a bank shot happens when one person bounces a message off a second person in order to deliver the message to the third person. Sometimes this is called triangulation. The bank shot is a favorite method of influence used by some members of every congregation. But we covenant to speak to one another directly: face-to-face.

If we have something to say that calls a person's actions into question, then we speak to that person face-to-face or in a phone conversation. If we wish to ask someone to do something that will require a great deal of effort or something that he or she would prefer not to do, we do it the same way. Face-to-face is best, of course, because that way we are able to use most effectively all of the nuances of speech and body language to communicate concern and vision while keeping our personal relationship alive, vital, and reconciled.

Finally, we remember that e-mail is a public document. What we may send innocently to one individual, expecting it to be read by that person alone, may be very easily forwarded to others, who in turn will forward it to still others. We say with e-mail only what we would put into the newspaper!

Thread Five   Clear Expectations: We Clarify Our Vision and What We Expect of One Another

We covenant to maintain a graceful and clear understanding of the vision we seek to accomplish together and what we expect of one another. Both are crucial to sound relationships and fellowship. Differing expectations can lead to frustration and disappointment. The team regularly reviews its covenantal agreements, which every team member is expected to observe and honor. Individual expectations for each team member may be clarified using three simple practices.

First, on an annual or semi-annual basis, as best fits our team life, we spend an extended period of time in ministry design. We think ahead about our vision and what steps to take next. During this time, each team member considers the personal steps he or she will take to fulfill the team goals. These steps may be shaped in conversation with the team leader as well as with others on the team. The defining vision and ministry practices of the congregation and the team will help to shape these steps. Such anticipated steps of each member need not be rigid expectations and requirements. We give one another the freedom and flexibility to modify next steps as new opportunities or unexpected obstacles present themselves.

Second, we keep our expectations clear by leading the team to think ahead on a monthly or quarterly basis, though not in as much detail as during the annual/semi-annual experience. The annual/semi-annual process looks at overall ministry design issues, whereas monthly/quarterly times of reflection deal with the daily realities of the ministry. It gives leaders and team members time to think ahead together and to stay together in thought and action. Simple questions guide the process: "How are we doing? Are we accomplishing what we anticipated? What have we learned? What help do we need? What are we going to do now?" The spirit of a time of thinking ahead is positive and encouraging. Recall God's word in Isaiah 43:19: "See, I am doing a new thing!" We look for the new thing, the next step in our ministry as a team and in our ministries as team members. Regular times of thinking ahead reclarify what is to be done and what kind of support may be required.

Third, we keep in touch with each other on a weekly basis. We can do this in informal conversations face-to-face, by the coffeepot, or on the phone. It is remarkable how much clarification and counsel may be offered in simple five-minute conversations. Such conversations may be informal, but they must be intentional. This check-up time is essential to sound leadership and warm *koinonia* fellowship. If misunderstandings develop or problems surface, we deal with them immediately. We don't save up our irritation for our next team meeting. We keep our relationships face-to-face, current, with all cards on the table. We work out problems between us and move ahead together.

Essential to the practice of clear expectations is that we don't surprise one another. We keep one another informed of our plans before we act or involve others. "No surprises" also means we respect one another enough to communicate thoroughly and to accept in a good spirit the possibility that some of our ideas for ministry will be modified. We let the team hear our plans first, directly from us, rather than indirectly from others. This is the practice of our team leader as well as the team members.

Thread Six   "Loose-Tight" Balance: We Serve Both with Freedom and within Boundaries

Think of a fleet of ships in which the admiral directs all ships to sail in formation. The looser the formation, the more freedom each ship has to set its own course. The tighter the formation, the less freedom each ship has to choose its own direction. This "loose-tight" concept is a useful way to consider the relationship between a team and its congregation and the relationship between team members and the team itself.[10]

For a ministry team, "loose" means that the congregation gives the

10. The "loose-tight" concept is discussed by Thomas J. Peters and Robert H. Waterman Jr. in *In Search of Excellence* (New York: Harper & Row, 1982).

team tremendous freedom to plan and carry out its vision for ministry. The congregation simply says to the team, "How can we help you or support you?" One of the strengths of ministry teams is that they are quite capable of self-direction. Teams given such latitude by their congregation can demonstrate astonishing levels of creativity.

"Tight" means that the team aligns its ministry with the defining vision and practices of the congregation. Every healthy congregation exerts appropriate authority in establishing its ministry boundaries by means of a defining vision that expresses why the congregation exists and what ministry practices it considers essential. Teams within congregational life align their life and ministry with those defining elements.

The "loose-tight" formula also applies to the relationship between team members and the team. With energetic, enthusiastic, responsible team members, we major in "loose." We give our team members all the freedom commensurate with their initiative and wisdom to carry out their responsibilities — as long as that ministry is consistent with the defining vision and practices of our team. "Loose" means that we respond to a member with dreams and energy by getting out of his way and giving permission: "Go to it. How can we help you or support you?" "Loose" can even mean, "We understand your plan, although we (or I) don't think we would do it that way, and here's why. But your plan is sound, and we want to back your ideas, so go to it, and let us know how we may support you." That's loose!

"Tight," on the other hand, means we or the team leader may ask you to do something you don't particularly want to do, or we may ask you not to do something you do want to do. When we ask for "tight," we explain why. We don't want to restrict one another's freedom on a whim. At the same time, we all realize that certain matters require stricter control. For example, we may ask that when members are driving to ministry activities, no more people get into a vehicle than there are seatbelts to accommodate them. With a guideline like that, it's possible that there would be an event for which there wouldn't be enough transportation. This is when the tightness of the reins is felt, but only because there could be very serious consequences if the guideline isn't followed.

Sometimes we may be inclined to be too "tight" because we're afraid that some team member will rock the boat or because the level of effort or risk involved in a certain endeavor will be high. We must constantly monitor ourselves and ask ourselves if such fear represents a truly significant concern. Sometimes it takes courage to be permission-giving and allow a team member to do something new, or allow the whole team to move in a new direction. Finding a healthy "loose-tight" balance is never easy, but it is essential.

Thread Seven   *Loving Loyalty: We Have the Freedom to Express*
             Differences of Opinion within the Team while
             Supporting Team Decisions to Those outside the Team

Loving loyalty means that out of love we stick together in public statements even when we disagree over an issue. We represent decisions as "our decisions" or "the staff's or elders' decision" or "the youth ministry team's decision." We don't say, "Some of us don't like it, but we're stuck with Jim and Janice's idea," thus "fingering" others and shifting all responsibility from ourselves.

We have to have the freedom to disagree within the team. Without it, our face-to-face relationships wouldn't be real. We want to be able to disagree agreeably and still model love, dignity, and unity to the congregation or wider ministry. Since our relationships are a demonstration of the Spirit of Jesus working within us, we have to practice a healthy "loose-tight" balance. That means respecting one another's dignity and blessing one another's vision even when we don't entirely agree, and showing unity, loyalty, and mutual respect and commitment to those who would feast on the conflict among leaders.

Using the "Good Report Principle," we speak well of another person even when we don't agree with him or her. Loving loyalty means we show honor and dignity to one another even when we don't agree or when others are critical of us or upset with our ministry.

We recognize that personal aims and approaches to ministry may change over time and that some among us may find our personal direction increasingly incongruent with the vision and practices of the team. Rather than practicing "loving loyalty" while enduring an increasing sense of dissonance with the team, these members have a perfect right to ask to be "sent" from the team, with our love and affection, to a new or different ministry.

Weaving the Threads Together: Building the Covenantal Agreements into Team Life

Adapt the seven threads to fit the needs of your own team or the ministry teams of your congregation. Weave each of these seven threads into the fabric of your team life. Model them. Encourage them. Use them as pathfinders to lead your team on the journey of becoming one in spirit and in mutual love. When you review them, do so with an eye toward growing in love for one another, experiencing "one heart," rather than establishing some sort of grading system with which to chastise each other. Talk about the seven threads as a team. Bring in supplementary material to enhance your knowledge and implementation of them.

I have found it useful for a ministry team to perform a self-examination of its experience of fellowship on a regular basis. Using a summary of the seven threads and other team courtesies,[11] I encourage every team to review its life together twice a year, typically at the beginning of the fall and again in early spring. Also explain the covenantal agreements to each new person joining the team and have your entire team review those agreements at this time. Just the process of discussing such agreements has a way of helping the team modify its behavior and build the maturity of its fellowship.

You can get a sense of how the team feels it's doing with each of the threads by giving every member a list of the seven threads with a five-point scale. (See the sample list on p. 116.) Ask them to anonymously assign a value for each thread, with "1" meaning "this thread is virtually non-existent in our team" and "5" indicating "our team practices this thread with excellence." Compute the team average for each thread. Then discuss the results together. Which threads are strong? Which are weaker and why? Celebrate your strengths, and talk about specific steps you can take to strengthen the weaker threads. Remember to maintain a positive tone during this review process. An ongoing, up-

---

11. A summary of this kind is found in Appendix One.

Spiritual Disciplines	I	2	3	4	5
Face-to-Face Relationships	I	2	3	4	5
Confidentiality	I	2	3	4	5
Communication	I	2	3	4	5
Clear Expectations	I	2	3	4	5
"Loose-Tight" Balance	I	2	3	4	5
Loving Loyalty	I	2	3	4	5

beat discussion of key issues concerning life together will help the team constantly reshape itself into the team Christ is calling it to be.[12]

Conclusion

If you want growing discipleship and warm fellowship, then with God's help and by his grace, you must make this a priority of your team life. It's a matter of team discipline and the establishment of patterns such as small-group life, shared meals, and prayer partnerships. Jesus said to his ministry team, "I have called you *friends*." Make the primary focus of ministry-team life the building of members in discipleship and friendship. The results will bless a great many other people as well.

12. For an in-depth assessment of many essential qualities of team life, see "The Team Readiness Survey" by Alan Roxburgh and Fred Romanuk of the Missional Leadership Institute: http://www.mliweb.net.

CHAPTER EIGHT

Fostering Team Discipleship

The ministry team's movement toward fellowship deepens as it pursues its movements upward in discipleship and outward in ministry. When I was involved in a college ministry team a number of years ago, Julie Johnson was a Purdue student who began to show evidence of her love for Christ and for people as she became involved in the ministry. We discerned her heart for ministry and invited her onto the team. She quickly became a part of our fellowship, getting to know us, sharing in meals and moments of laughter with us, and sharing in the caring for one another. In the months that followed, Julie began to grow in her service as a team member. She led a small group of students and also met with students in one-to-one interpersonal ministry. As she participated in the life of the team, I watched her faith develop in its depth and maturity. Julie also had the gift of teaching, and she began to excel at that. Eventually she led that entire student ministry. Today she is the national director of the Spirituality Program at Columbia Theological Seminary in Atlanta.

All of the members of a ministry team will, in different ways, grow in discipleship and personal ministry, as Julie did, as they participate in the team's small-group life and accept service responsibilities in accord with their interests and gifts. Some team members will have more heart for interpersonal ministry, others more passion for the tasks to be accomplished, but all of them will be encouraged to develop and share in a vibrant discipleship, one that is pulsing with life and energy.

Some years ago, Peter Benson and Carolyn Eklin undertook a major study of faith development, loyalty, and congregational life involving six Protestant denominations — about 11,000 individuals and 561 congregations. Among their many sobering conclusions was this: "Only a minority of Protestant adults evidence the kind of integrated, vibrant, and life-encompassing faith congregations seek to develop. For most adults, faith is underdeveloped, lacking some of the key elements necessary for faith maturity."[1] In *Growing True Disciples*, George Barna draws the same conclusion from extensive polling data.[2]

One thing is clear. Without spiritually vital people, we will not have a vital church. You may have an active church, a busy ministry, even a large one. But genuine vitality requires the participation of spiritually alive people who have the heart and will to see others grow in their spiritual lives as well.

Growing Disciples

I was in high school during the days that the music of the Beatles zoomed to the top of the charts. For an entire semester my French teacher replaced the tapes of the French language we were supposed to listen to with Beatles' music. I didn't learn much French that year — although I sure learned a lot of Beatles' songs! Looking back, I now realize that my teacher must have been experiencing some job burnout. This is a humorous example, but I think it makes a good point. If we really want to be catalysts for the spiritual growth of others, we don't want to discover we've been giving them Beatles' music when they needed French. We must understand what defines both the content and the means of growth in discipleship so that we know what we're aiming for in the lives of people and how, by the grace of God, to go about it.

Our growth as disciples, our spiritual formation, results from our relationship with God in and through Jesus Christ and involves all of the life experiences, attitudes, and behaviors that flow from that relationship. Spiritual formation is not a set of rather vague "feelings" or opinions about various spiritual experiences. It is the total life change that results from faith in the trinitarian God and obedience to that

---

1. Peter Benson and Carolyn Eklin, *Effective Christian Education: A National Study of Protestant Congregations* (Minneapolis: Search Institute, 1990), pp. 3-4.

2. George Barna, *Growing True Disciples* (Colorado Springs: WaterBrook Press, 2001).

God's will as it is revealed to us in Scripture. "My dear children, for whom I am again in the pains of childbirth *until Christ is formed in you . . .*" (Gal. 4:19, my emphasis). "It is he whom we proclaim, warning everyone and teaching everyone in all wisdom, so that we may present everyone mature in Christ" (Col. 1:28, NRSV). Discipleship is growing in a new life that is entirely the gift of grace and that reflects the character and will of God as well as the experience of knowing our loving and present God in every moment of life. It is literally the process of becoming like Jesus, a process formally known as sanctification.

When the Apostle Paul speaks of presenting every person complete or mature in Christ, he uses the significant Greek word *teleios*. The root of this word is *tele*, as in *tele*scope, meaning the end of something, the conclusion of an act, the result. *Teleios* means complete, whole, mature, grown up. "He who began a good work in you will carry it on to completion [*teleios*] until the day of Christ Jesus" (Phil. 1:6). A disciple when fully grown is *teleios*, like the teacher.

An excellent way for a ministry team to grow disciples is to join in the practice of spiritual disciplines in accord with the first of the Seven Threads.[3] By using such disciplines for enabling spiritual growth, we may cooperate with the work of the Holy Spirit in one another's life. Our role is to function as God's loving instruments of grace. In the spirit of *koinonia* fellowship we say to one another on the team, "I am with you. Let's grow in Christ together."

Using Biblical Patterns as Defining Practices for Developing Discipleship

Scripture tells us how to grow in discipleship with its many exhortations such as "Encourage one another," "Love one another," and "Be

3. Outstanding treatments of the practice of spiritual disciplines include Richard Foster, *Celebration of Discipline* (San Francisco: Harper & Row, 1988); Glenn W. McDonald, *The Disciplemaking Church: From Dry Bones to Spiritual Vitality* (Grand Haven, Mich.: FaithWalk Publishing, 2004); Greg Ogden, *Discipleship Essentials: A Guide to Building Your Life in Christ* (Downers Grove, Ill.: InterVarsity Press, 1998); John Ortberg, *The Life You've Always Wanted* (Grand Rapids: Zondervan, 2002); and Dallas Willard, *The Spirit of the Disciplines* (San Francisco: HarperCollins, 1991).

prepared to give an answer for the hope within you." Scripture also shows us how to grow in discipleship in its many descriptions of people engaged in the practice of ministry. We see Jesus meeting with the Twelve (which shows us small groups), the picture of the early church in Acts 2:42 (where we read, "They devoted themselves to the apostles' teaching and to the fellowship, to the breaking of bread, and to prayer"), and Barnabas and Paul (which shows us apprenticing). The patterns for developing discipleship that we discover in Scripture are pictures of ministry, pictures that show us defining practices that we may apply to our own ministries today in cooperation with the ministry of the Holy Spirit. Think of the biblical pattern of encouragement, for example, and instantly you have the mental picture of a warm smile in a difficult moment, a phone call offering encouraging words, a hug given to a person who's grieving.

There are dozens of biblical patterns for ministry. I have found that six defining practices of transformational ministry embrace whole domains of ministry behaviors. Each of the six may be used in the life of a ministry team to foster discipleship among its own members and among those whom the team serves in its ministry. These same patterns may also be used to shape activities of a ministry team and the program it leads. In addition, individuals may use these patterns in ministry to their family, friends, and others in their life, especially because ministry is first a lifestyle to be lived before it is a program to be run. These six defining practices of transformational ministry — of developing discipleship — are Witness, Prayer, Care, Word, "With me," and Send.[4]

The Defining Practice of Witness

Many American Christians today are reluctant to speak about their faith in personal conversations, even when given an obvious opportunity to do so. Ministry-team life offers a wonderful opportunity for its members to learn this precious habit.

An interesting phrase in the New Testament contains the words of

4. See my books entitled *The Vibrant Church* (Ventura, Calif.: Regal Books, 1989), and *Twelve Dynamic Shifts for Transforming Your Church* (Grand Rapids: Eerdmans, 2002).

the witness "what we have seen and heard." In Acts 4:20 we read, "For we cannot help speaking about what we have seen and heard." In Acts 22:15 we read, "You will be his witness to all men of what you have seen and heard." When we bear witness, we speak of what we ourselves have seen and heard — the good news about Jesus Christ that we hear in Scripture, and God's work, which we see in daily lives. Bearing witness is basic to nurturing discipleship in others (and in ourselves) because it offers both the call to faith in Jesus Christ and reinforces that faith with affirmations of God's love and presence. Indeed, the very act of bearing witness has a wonderful way of confirming our own faith and renewing our own passion for God.

I once participated in a ministry team which led a large Bible study for adults and met every Friday noon to nurture its own small-group life and to plan its ministry. During one of its meetings, a woman named Joan, a professor of nursing at a nearby university, shared with the team that her father was facing major surgery the next day. She said, "I'm concerned because insofar as I know, he has never professed faith in Jesus Christ." We talked for a while, and someone asked, "If you're going to phone him tonight, why don't you simply ask him directly about his faith?" That night Joan called her dad. Because of her nursing background, her father asked her several questions about the surgery and about his prospects for recovery. After giving him answers, Joan commented, "Dad, you've asked me a number of questions, and now I have one for you: Have you ever received Jesus Christ into your life?" There was a silence, and then her father replied, "No, I never have. But you know, I was planning on doing it tomorrow!" Joan responded, "Dad, is there any reason that you should wait until tomorrow?" When he said no, Joan asked, "Dad, would you like it if I prayed a prayer right over the phone, and you could pray with me and ask Christ into your life?" Her father answered, "Yes, I would!" That night Joan experienced the joy and privilege of leading her father to faith in Christ — over the phone. His surgery was a success, and he went on to become an enthusiastic follower of Jesus Christ.

Bearing witness offers testimony concerning the reality of God's love and the good news of Jesus Christ to both the Christian and the non-Christian. During a ministry team's small-group life, members learn to bear witness to the reality of God's presence in their lives. In their ministry they bear witness to Jesus Christ to the people they serve and, when appropriate, offer a call to faith, the invitation to believe in and follow him.

The Defining Practice of Prayer

The Apostle Paul says, "Christ Jesus, who died — more than that, who was raised to life — is at the right hand of God and *is also interceding for us*" (Rom. 8:34, my emphasis; see also Heb. 7:25). If Jesus lives to pray on our behalf, so ought we to pray on one another's behalf. When a ministry team prays, its members are relying on the most basic of ministry principles: that the Holy Spirit is the author of spiritual growth. Team members pray for each other's well-being and for growth in discipleship. Well-being prayers include prayers for a person's health, relationships, and work, as well as for the health of the fellowship, the surrounding city, and the world. I call those kinds of prayers *shalom* prayers, "that it might be well with you." Discipleship prayers — what I call *teleios* prayers — ask God to enable a person to grow in faith, to grow in the image of Jesus Christ, to become the person God wants her to be. Think, for example, of the prayer life of Epaphras described in Colossians 4:12: "Epaphras, who is one of you and a servant of Christ Jesus, sends greetings. He is always wrestling in prayer for you, that you may stand firm in all the will of God, mature [*teleios*] and fully assured." Although Epaphras may have prayed "shalom" prayers for the Colossians, here he was clearly interested in praying for their discipleship and spiritual maturity.

Since American culture is a culture of busyness that is not conducive to the lifestyle of prayer, the team deliberately encourages its members to practice the spiritual discipline of prayer. They learn to serve others by praying for them. They pray individually in their homes and together when the team engages in small-group "Word-Share-Prayer." One reason why prayer partnerships are a useful spiritual discipline for teams is that they give individual members a pattern and a motivation for developing personal prayer lives in their homes. A useful method a team may use is to pray through a list of those people in the ministry it leads or serves. Invite team members to pray for the people on the list, person by person, as a part of their daily devotional life. If the list is long, then suggest they divide it up and pray through the whole list weekly or monthly. Simply pray for growing spiritual maturity and for personal well-being for each person.

God works in powerful ways among his people when they engage in systematic prayer for each other and for the people to whom they minister — not deferring the responsibility for prayer to those special people or teams who have a particular interest in prayer. In this way, the practice of intercessory prayer is shared across the life of the congregation.

The Defining Practice of Care

When David was in a particularly difficult situation, his friend Jonathan came and "helped him find strength in God" (1 Sam. 23:16). This is as it should be, since Scripture instructs us to "bear one another's burdens" (Gal. 6:2). We are agents of the love of God in each other's lives, doing whatever we can do to make that love real and meaningful. When my mom called to say that my dad had died, a member of my ministry team drove me to the airport. The experience was so intense that I don't even remember who it was — only that the team cared, and I felt the love of God in a difficult moment. When facing another situation that I found intimidating, a member of my team sought me out. He looked into my eyes and said, "Be not afraid," and with his encouragement I shifted my trust to the God who is with us and was thus able to cope with the situation. Team life creates an environment for spiritual growth when team members care for each other. When someone is in need, we show up and show that we care.

For Jesus Christ, caring for people and nurturing them as disciples went hand in hand. He clearly recognized that people are not "objects" to be gathered for a ministry task and then simply dismissed when the goal is met or the meeting is over. When, after a long day, Jesus finished teaching the five thousand, he could have dismissed them like a professor dismissing a class. He could simply have said, "Go home" — which is exactly what his disciples suggested. Instead, he fed them, thus meeting their physical needs as well as their spiritual needs. Follow his example. Be alert to the needs of the people you are seeking to nurture and take steps to address them. As Robert Schuller says, "Find a need and fill it. Find a hurt and heal it."

We practice care intentionally; we don't assume that it will just happen. Guided by the team leader and the leadership core, team members make a conscious effort to show care and concern for each other in Christ's name.

The Defining Practice of Imparting the Word

When the Apostle Paul spoke to the Thessalonian church, he described Scripture as "the word of God, which is at work in you who believe" (1 Thess. 2:13). Indeed, the Word and the Holy Spirit are the primary instruments of spiritual growth. The more you impart the knowledge and understanding of Scripture to people and the more you get them into Scripture, the more they will grow in Christ. A twenty-minute sermon once a week can hardly compete with the crush of information and philosophy that our media-dense culture beams at every person every day. To grow disciples of your team members, find creative ways to engage them in earnest Bible study by means of team discussion, personal study and devotions, and the hearing of the Word preached. Engaging the team in study using one of the many excellent study guides now available, motivating them to do some text memorization, and studying books on Christian life and ministry are other fruitful means of imparting the Word.

One of my most vivid experiences of ministry-team life grew out of a year-long study of Luke's Gospel. Our assignment each week was to study a chapter of Luke and write down every illustration, every picture, every principle and pattern of ministry — everything we observed Jesus doing to nurture disciples. Then during our team meeting time we really dug into the text together, sharing our insights and getting increasingly excited about the implications of each chapter for our own ministry.

If a team becomes so agenda-driven and task-driven that meaningful engagement of the Word is consistently set aside or paid only the briefest attention, then the team loses a powerful catalyst for spiritual growth. Although it may call itself a "ministry team," it is actually no more than a functional committee.

The Defining Practice of the "With Me" Principle

The most effective way to get the Word into people is by studying it *with* them, which leads us to the next principle of growth: the "with me" principle. In Mark 3:14 we read, "He appointed twelve — designating them apostles — that they might be *with* him and that he might send them out to preach" (my emphasis). Jesus was constantly asking people to be with him, to follow him, to be where he was. We use the "with me" principle ourselves when we invite others to join us in whatever we're doing for the purpose of growing as friends and as followers of Christ and for doing ministry together. Team life itself is in fact a complex expression of the "with me" principle.[5]

Using the with-me principle, I would invite a person or two on my ministry team with whom I wanted to grow in Christ to go with me to hear a Christian speaker or concert. I would ask them to come with me to worship, to a Sunday School class, or to a small-group Bible study. I would invite them to join me in whatever I'm doing, just as Jesus invited his disciples to be with him in whatever he was doing. Thus we will grow as friends and as followers of Christ.

Ministry teams use the with-me principle every time they invite a new person to join the team or to join with them in the team's ministry. When I was a graduate student, I attended the Covenant Presbyterian Church in West Lafayette, Indiana. I was a member of an evangelism ministry team with the pastor of the church, Jim Tozer. He was a very busy man and had little time to meet. Then he realized that he visited patients in the hospital each week by himself. He began using the with-me principle by taking me along, not to teach me how to visit people in the hospital (though I did learn that with him) but to include me in his life and to give us time together to experience and to discuss life

5. For an extensive treatment of the "with me" principle, see my book entitled *The Joy of Discipling* (Grand Rapids: Zondervan, 1989), now available from www.vitalfaithresources .com.

and ministry. As a result, we developed a real relationship and a dear friendship, and eventually I was to work for him for many years.

I learned from Jim's example. I constantly ask myself, "What am I doing that I might ask another team member to do with me? How can I encourage others on the team to include people *with* them in what they're doing?" This is significant because within the context of with-me time, deep face-to-face relationships grow, and we experience real *koinonia* fellowship.

Scott Stevens, the former director of youth ministries in the congregation I serve, once shared with me that he was thinking of attending an upcoming youth conference at Willow Creek in Chicago. I said, "I'm delighted that you're going, Scott. You'll get some great ideas. Don't forget the with-me principle. Take Tina [his wife] with you if you can, so you grow together, and take some of your youth leaders too, so that your team gets a vision together." Scott went with Tina and took six youth leaders "with him." The with-me principle changed their lives and their ministry.

Use the with-me principle in your leisure time too as a means of focusing on team members. Going to the movies? Ask a teammate to go with you. Going out for ice cream or to see fireworks or some other event? Take someone with you. Real relationships don't grow simply by attending church and ministry meetings with people. They grow as you share in all the experiences of life.

Consider all of the other resources available to you in encouraging the growth of team members. If you are a team leader, take the team to various equipping seminars and inspirational events or on field trips to see other ministries pursuing a vision similar to yours. A simple overnight team retreat can be the essence of the with-me principle because the team devotes itself to "Word-Share-Prayer," planning, sharing meals, and enjoying time together, all of which can have a tremendously positive impact on spiritual growth.

The Defining Practice of Sending to Ministry

Jesus said to his followers, "As the Father has *sent* me, I am *sending* you" (John 20:21, my emphasis). And it's worth repeating the verse I quoted above in this context: "He appointed twelve — designating them apostles — that they might be *with* him and that he might *send* them out to preach" (Mark 3:14, my emphasis). Using the "send" principle, we work to connect people to ministries of their own and to other people they will help nurture, and to the use of their spiritual gifts in service. People grow when they help others grow. Few activities are more conducive to spiritual growth than serving others. No wonder Jesus was always engaged in ministry *to* people *with* people. Those whom he mobilized for ministry with him were the ones who developed most significantly in discipleship. Despite this powerful example, the church has not excelled in this matter of sending and mobilizing its members for ministry. Ministry teams can help overcome this weakness by sending their members to ministry in two different though related ministries — to ministry as personal lifestyle and to ministry as fulfillment of a particular responsibility.

In ministry as lifestyle, we use all six defining practices for fostering discipleship. For example, I bear witness to my family and to those to whom I am ministering by speaking of the reality of God and the person of Jesus Christ in my life. I pray well-being and discipleship prayers for them. I look for appropriate ways to care for them, impart the Word to them, intentionally spend time with them, and discern ways to engage (send) them to their own ministry.

In ministry that fulfills a responsibility, we engage in task accomplishment by using our spiritual gifts, abilities, and interests. When I was a graduate student at Purdue and still fairly new to the Christian faith, a friend by the name of Bob Pickett called to say that he had been scheduled to preach at a small rural church the following Sunday. The church was without a pastor, and Bob was one of the guest speakers they invited to preach the Word. Bob was calling to see if I would preach that weekend too. Preach? I was both excited and terrified by the idea — but I said yes. That Sunday remains one of my most vivid experiences of ministry. Bob saw something in me that I hadn't seen. In "sending" me to ministry, he helped me discern and begin to use one of my own spiritual gifts. In a similar way, a ministry team works to connect each team member with the ministry roles and responsibilities that most effectively use his or her gifts, interests, experiences, and abilities.

Since the team member is called on to offer interpersonal ministry to others and to exercise spiritual gifts, training in both is essential. A key skill of interpersonal ministry is that of developing disciples: knowing how to pray for and with others, how to share the faith, how to lead others in Bible study, and how to use the with-me principle. Other key skills include showing care (during times of grief, illness, and uncertainty), helping people identify their places in ministry, effective faith-sharing, and small-group leadership.

Team-member training must also include whatever each member needs in order to become proficient in the use of his or her spiritual gifts. Team leaders also need further training in matters such as how to best understand and implement principles of organization, how to increase vision, how to plan ministry, how to develop disciples, and how to grow leaders. Providing this training is one of the ways congregations and ministries can best assist their teams in development.

Using the Defining Practices to Develop Team Members into Disciples

In many congregations the pastor is viewed as the primary practitioner of interpersonal ministry, while the "lay" people merely run and attend activities. A great power of the ministry team is that simply by participating in team life, its members develop the skills of interpersonal ministry.

The reason the ministry team can be such an effective developer of disciples is that team life incorporates all six defining practices of fostering discipleship. Team members bear witness to each other of the reality of God's love and power. They pray for and care for one another, learn the Word together, and spend time "with" one another. They also send one another to ministry. Committees that center their existence solely on task accomplishment are using only the practice of "send to ministry," just as classes that meet solely for teaching the Word are emphasizing only that single practice. It is true that committee members will experience some spiritual growth as they serve, but not nearly the kind of growth they would enjoy if they had been nurtured in a context emphasizing all six practices. This explains why the committee-based church isn't going to see the same level of discipleship among its people as the team-based congregation will.

Since ministry teams incorporate all six defining practices of disciple-making ministry, they are *discipling fellowships*. As such, they enable the church to become a discipling congregation as their number increases throughout the overall life of the church. Thus ministry teams decentralize the disciple-growing function of a congregation. Developing discipleship is no longer the primary responsibility of the pastor or the Christian education committee. Every team grows disciples.

The team uses the six defining practices to guide its own team life and to guide the ministry it leads. For example, suppose the team leads a group of college students. Team members use the six practices to guide their own fellowship as well as their interpersonal ministry to the students. The team also figures out how to use the defining practices to design program initiatives so that the activities of the group will include witness, prayer, care, engagement of the Word, and sending members of the group to minister to still others.

Another reason the ministry team is such an effective disciple-growing environment is that it combines both the class model and the mentor model of instruction. Traditional Christian educational activities such as Sunday School, Vacation Bible School, and various classes for adults are based on the class model. This model, which typically features one teacher leading the class, is the primary method of instruction in America — in education, in business, and in the church. The class model of teaching typically delivers information without relationship: the teacher often doesn't know the students personally. But Jesus himself showed us that the class model can be a very effective one for teaching and encouragement. Jesus used the class model in teaching larger groups such as those who gathered to hear the Sermon on the Mount and the crowd that packed a house so tightly that a hole had to be cut in the roof to lower a paralytic down to him. The class model very definitely has a place in our ministries as well. Last Sunday I attended a worship service with two thousand people, only four of whom I knew personally. Nevertheless, the sermon, a "teaching" based on Isaiah 6, was well delivered and helpful to me.

Another effective approach to teaching is the mentor model, which involves a master teacher who spends significant teaching time in the company of relatively few learners. This is the model that Socrates used with Plato, the approach that a master craftsman uses to teach a few apprentices. The mentor model informs the patterns of the American graduate-school system, in which a professor spends a great deal of time with his small group of graduate students.

The approach to teaching that Jesus used most frequently was a marvelous mix of the class model and the mentor model. He had his apprentices, the Twelve, with whom he shared deep and close friendships. He taught them in depth and modeled his way of living to them. Jesus Christ also addressed "classes" of "students" — groups and crowds of people with whom he experienced virtually no personal relationship but to whom he imparted significant messages. When he was teaching those groups or "classes," his ministry team was with him, so he engaged in the class model and the mentor model simultaneously.

Those few who were closest to him received the greatest learning opportunity, while the larger group or "class" also benefited from his teaching. Recall that after Jesus told the Parable of the Sower (Mark 4) to a crowd, the apostles took the opportunity to ask Jesus to go into more depth in a private session much like a ministry-team meeting. Remember too that Jesus never allowed the few to be passive participants when he addressed the larger crowd. Rather, he ministered to the many with the few. The feeding of the five thousand is a classic illustration of this principle.

To see Jesus Christ's teaching is to see the power of combining both the mentor and the class models — which we can see in the ministry team. The team experiences fellowship with the leader and with one another, and the team engages in ministry together. It is the whole of these experiences that fosters the most significant discipleship growth.

Jesus Christ not only made time for his team; he made time with them his top priority. These were the people who most deeply absorbed his teaching and who grew as they learned to minister to others. As an engaging and electrifying speaker, Jesus could easily have contented himself with the "lecture circuit" and been satisfied with the results, but he wasn't! He made the few as important to his ministry as the many. The genius of his teaching ministry is that he gave additional focus to those few without neglecting the many. In the same way, if you serve in depth with the few on your ministry team, you will multiply your impact on the group the team is serving, and you too may focus on a few while reaching the many. The ministry team will share the ministry to the group, and they in turn will advance significantly in their own growth.

Conclusion

The defining practices for fostering discipleship are not simply a short-hand method of describing the ministry of Jesus or the characteristics of team life. They are a template for ministry meant to be used in the design and practice of team ministry, both at the interpersonal level and at the level of patterning our activities and our programs. If we faithfully follow these practices, we will reap rich rewards.

CHAPTER NINE

Guiding the Team in Ministry to People

In the accomplishment of the triple extension movement of disciple-ship, fellowship, and ministry, the effective ministry team adds a significant aspect to its ministries often missed by the more task-oriented committee and board. Such teams attend to both persons and tasks in a double focus of ministry. Thus a Sunday School class ministry team focuses on each student individually, *and* the team attends to the many administrative and teaching tasks involved in conducting the class. A clothing-drive team may not know the specific needs of the individual people they seek to serve, but they lift them up in prayer, aware of them as real people, while also attending to the details of the clothing drive itself. Task-oriented service projects tend to center strictly on the job to be done. The double focus of ministry brings relational and task balance to the team's practice of ministry: tending the individual sheep (people) while leading the whole flock (program).

In this chapter I will address the people focus of the ministry team, and in the next chapter I will address the accomplishment of the vision for which the team was called into being. A balanced ministry team keeps one eye on the people to whom it is in ministry and the other eye on the work to be accomplished.

Understanding the Importance of People-Focused Ministry

Every ministry team should remain focused on the people it serves. Even if a team has a very specific task assignment, as will a Habitat for

Humanity team, a stewardship team, or a kitchen ministry team, it can remain people-responsive while it also attends to its task responsibilities. Unfortunately, it is very common for a team whose primary responsibility is a group of people — such as a ministry to men, women, or children, or a fellowship of college students — to find itself spending all of its time in program and task-related decisions and neglecting paying specific attention to the people involved or potentially involved, except those cases requiring special pastoral care.

When a team relies solely on the activities it leads to minister to the people in a group, then everyone gets treated the same way. Those who participate in the team's "program" experience the program together: "Come hear our guest speaker"; "Join us for a Lenten series on the Cross"; "Sign up for the retreat." This is "batch processing," whole-group programming that offers everyone the same experience. Don't get me wrong. There is an essential place for this in ministry. When activities are well conceived and attuned to the needs and particulars of a given group, they can be extremely effective in nurturing discipleship. Just think of the last worship service you attended that spoke to your heart, and you know this is true. When a team attends to whole-group programming elements by carefully making task assignments, then by God's grace it can make a significant impact on the people in the group. So just imagine how much greater an impact such a team can have when it is also paying attention to the discipleship and compassion needs of every individual in the group as well.

People-responsive ministry is not the sole province of pastors or ministry leaders; it is the desired objective of every team member of every ministry team in the congregation. Every team, whether leading a group or accomplishing a specific task, works to balance its awareness of both people and programmatic concerns. Let's look at the ministry team's focus on people in two areas: interpersonal ministry and small-group life.

Engaging in Interpersonal Ministry

In the congregation I serve, Bob and Mary LaTurner were members of a ministry team who met every Friday at noon to consider how best to lead "The Gathering" Bible study, a group of a hundred people that met at the church on Wednesday night. The Gathering began its meetings with a brief time of worship and music, followed by a forty-minute lecture on a passage of Scripture. During that hour everyone there had the same whole-group experiences. Immediately following that large-group meeting, members drove to one of a dozen homes to participate in "Word-Share-Prayer" small groups that met until 9:30 or 10:00 that night.

During a typical ministry-team meeting, Bob and Mary, along with the other team members, each accepted one or two follow-through contacts. These involved things like phoning to welcome a new visitor to The Gathering or asking a regular participant to join a small group. In addition, follow-through often meant touching base with someone who was ill or absent just to express warmth and concern.

The LaTurners also led one of the small groups that met after the large-group Bible study. They carried on an extensive interpersonal ministry to the people in their group. For example, when a new couple, Tom and Janet Meade, began to attend the large-group meeting on Wednesday night, Bob and Mary invited them into their own small group. Tom first professed his faith in Jesus Christ during a meeting of that small group. When he was diagnosed with cancer, Bob drove him from Indiana to Arizona to fulfill Tom's lifelong dream of seeing the Grand Canyon.

Bob and Mary clearly had the gift of hospitality. Mary was constantly looking for ways to make new people feel welcome, so her role on the ministry team was, naturally, hospitality. She led a small ministry team of others from "The Gathering" fellowship to think through and initiate hospitality events, which she and Bob hosted in their own home and in a variety of other places.

They were fully engaged ministry-team members. They offered a multilevel interpersonal ministry and undertook task assignments appropriate to their interests and gifts. When they first joined the team, of course, they didn't start out with this scope of ministry. As new ministry-team members they were asked to do only some follow-through work with individuals. They were given more assignments when their particular spiritual gifts and appropriate serving roles surfaced.

A ministry team that leads a group — whether it's made up of men, women, young people, couples, or singles — functions in the same way during group meetings *and* between meetings: by focusing on people, by loving and serving people even when program duties have been completed. Mary and Bob are wonderful examples of that.

Developing Interpersonal Ministry Skills

When Jesus said, "As the Father has sent me, I am sending you," do you suppose the disciples thought they were being sent to run programs? Obviously there were organizational issues involved, such as the issues that surfaced in the controversy over the care of the widows that we read about in chapter six of Acts. At the same time, we see in the lives of Jesus and his disciples the practice of intense interpersonal ministry. We can find a description of it in First Thessalonians: "But we were gentle among you, like a mother caring for her little children. . . . For you know that we dealt with each of you as a father deals with his own children, encouraging, comforting and urging you to live lives worthy of God, who calls you into his kingdom and glory" (2:7, 11-12). Clearly, when Jesus "sent" the disciples, he was sending them directly to people.

It's one thing to be in charge of a program assignment like "publicity." It's quite another to be involved with people personally. Many of us are unskilled in this practice and so find ourselves uneasy at the prospect of having direct interpersonal involvement with the spiritual lives of others. We simply leave it up to the pastor and a few others who are trained to do it. We know Jesus said to his disciples, "Follow me and I will make you fishers of people," but we haven't really made the concept real in our own lives, assuming that was meant for the Twelve and other "professional" Christians.

If we find ourselves at this crossroads, we would do well to remember Luke 6:40, a golden text of discipleship: "A student is not above his teacher, but everyone who is fully trained will be like his teacher." Jesus certainly handled "program concerns." Think of Palm Sunday: some pre-arrangements had been made to procure a colt for him to ride before the two disciples were sent to fetch it. Yet, when we think of Jesus' ministry, we think first of his interpersonal ministry — to Nicodemus, the woman at the well, and Zacchaeus, to name just a few examples. So it must be with us if we would grow to be like our Teacher. Interpersonal ministry is a defining practice of the team-based church, a fundamental matter for every ministry team and ultimately every member. Interpersonal ministry can be a growing part of our ministry if we trust Christ to help us and begin to learn some new patterns of interaction.

As in any new endeavor, we will need encouragement, patience, and some skill training in order to engage in interpersonal ministry. Think of a mother or a father with children at home. It's easy for a parent at any stage of life to wonder if he or she has the skills necessary to guide those children at that particular point in time. Yet dedicated parents don't for a moment let those worries stop them from becoming the best parents they can be. They take who they are, what they know, and what they have, and they put all of it to use to the best of their God-given ability to love and develop their children as followers of Jesus Christ and mature human beings. This is the essence of interpersonal ministry: taking what God has given us and reproducing it in the lives of the people in our ministries.

The team leader along with the leadership core works to develop the experience and skill level of team members with respect to interpersonal ministry by engaging them directly in ministry and by inviting the team to equipping/learning opportunities designed to "grow" ministry skills. The team-based congregation can assist the development of the interpersonal ministry skills of all its teams' members by offering regular workshops, seminars, and other learning opportunities geared to equip people in the "how-to's" of interpersonal ministry.

Some members of a ministry team will be more gifted than others in these sorts of interpersonal practices. A person with the gift of mercy will have a greater ability to help people cope and to be present in times of grief. A person with the gift of evangelism will have more facility in faith sharing, and so on. Still, virtually everyone on the team can develop some competency in these practices. My own gifts are stronger in the areas of administration and teaching than in the area of mercy, yet through small-group life I have learned to be reasonably effective in offering care. Those on a team with a particular spiritual gift or facility can help the rest of us learn how.

For this reason, when identifying and inviting people to join a group ministry team, look for those people who have indicated a willingness to pursue interpersonal ministry as well as a willingness to assume task responsibility to fulfill the team's ministry vision. Such people help the team make the double focus of ministry one of its defining practices. Recall the Apostle Paul's comment to the Thessalonian church: "We loved you so much that we were delighted to share with you not only the gospel of God *but our lives as well,* because you had become so dear to us" (1 Thess. 2:8, my emphasis).

Employing the Defining Practices for Fostering Discipleship

The six defining practices for fostering discipleship that a team uses to develop its own members are also used by team members both in interpersonal ministry and in program design for the group they lead. The team uses its planning times to reflect on ways to ensure that every member of the group they lead is encouraged to grow as a Christian witness, to have a prayer life on behalf of others, to be engaged in the study of the Word, to participate in fellowship (by the practice of care and the "with me" principle), and to be "sent" to a particular ministry assignment.

Employing the Practices of Attending and Connecting

Two additional useful practices that ministry-team members may use to expand their interpersonal ministry *during* the meeting of their group are attending and connecting.

Attending means paying deliberate attention to people who are alone or new or in some way appear to be unconnected during the meeting. Attending is the simple practice of zeroing in on someone for conversation. To attend is to make a person your "ministry for the meeting" — to greet her, introduce her to others, sit with her, invite her back, invite her to join a small group, and so on. Find out a little about her. Make her feel welcome. Answer questions she may have about the ministry. Team members do this in two's, asking another group member in "with me" fashion to go and greet someone.

Let's say you see a person you don't know walk into the room before the meeting begins. You say to a friend, "Marty, let's go talk to her." You walk over and say, "Welcome, we're glad you're here." "Thank you," she replies, "I'm glad to be here." After you introduce yourselves, you continue to engage her in conversation, perhaps introducing her to a few others. You sit near her during the meeting. Afterward you continue to connect her with others and say, "I'm looking forward to seeing you next week." That's attending.

When several members of a ministry team attend to someone new both before and after the meeting, that person begins to think, "There's a place for me here." As this example shows, attending is not something only the most conversational and outgoing people can do. All of us can grab a friend and make someone welcome.

Often team members are inclined to come to the group meeting and speak only to their good friends, as though this is the only time they'll see them. Use this basic axiom: "Ministry in public; friendship in private." In other words, in the public arena, the team members focus on those who need someone to attend to them. Say hello to your friends, but don't focus on them unless they're in genuine need. You'll be seeing them again soon enough.

Connecting is another interpersonal ministry method used to greet a newcomer or someone standing alone. Engage her in conversation, then connect her to someone who is already a part of the fellowship and ease yourself out of their conversation so you are free to connect to someone else. "Marty Lawson, meet Janice Anderson. Janice, I understand that Marty has many of the same interests in Sunday School that you do." As soon as the two of them begin to talk, you quietly withdraw. That's connecting.

Connecting people with people is actually the role of a good host welcoming guests into his or her home. The key here is to grasp who the host is and is not. The host isn't the pastor or group leader. The host is every member of the ministry team. As a matter of fact, as the congregation begins to learn the skills of interpersonal ministry, they come to know that each and every one of them is a host whenever the fellowship gathers. A host is familiar with the group, knows many of the people, and works to connect people who are new or don't know very many others. In a similar way, Jesus Christ is always the Host in the gatherings of his people. All of us are called to act on his behalf by connecting the people present at any gathering.

The practice of connecting may seem simple to you, but to someone who's "unconnected," it's very important. It says to a person, "We're more than just a friendly group that just says, 'Hi, how are you, welcome to our program, see you, bye!' We're hospitable. We want you to come into our life, and you're genuinely welcome among us. We want to get to know you." During such attending and connecting times, team members have the chance to get to know people, become more aware of their needs and interests, and invite them to join small groups and consider opportunities for service.

What happens at a typical ministry event? Beforehand the participants mill around, talking only to friends and acquaintances. When the meeting begins, they often sit passively in rows, listening to the "program." They have come to receive rather than to give themselves in interpersonal ministry to others. Afterwards they get up and mill around again, connecting with friends again before leaving. In this context, people tend to leave interpersonal ministry to the pastor, teacher, or leader of the group. Since this person is often consumed by program details, he or she is often too busy to practice attending and connecting. Furthermore, someone with a special need, question, or concern commonly takes up most of the leader's "face-to-face" time, so that he or she is effectively "neutralized" when it comes to speaking with many others.

However — and this is a *big* however — when a ministry team comes to a gathering prepared to focus on people, suddenly there are five, ten, or more people in addition to the leader/teacher/pastor able to offer the interpersonal ministry of attending and connecting. Now there are that many more people caring for others. The leader may be monopolized by a particular person, but the interpersonal ministry not only continues but also touches far more people than the leader ever could alone. Such interpersonal ministry is not the province of "greeters" assigned to meet people briefly as they walk in the door. It is the practice of every team member.

Engaging in Follow-Through

We saw how Bob and Mary LaTurner carried out various interactions with group members as part of a group leadership team. These interactions included welcoming new visitors, offering encouragement to the sick, and inviting individuals into a small-group Bible study. Follow-through is what the team does in response to the particular needs and opportunities for ministry that the individuals in a group present to them. The team makes follow-through a deliberate part of its team meetings by regularly reviewing the individual needs and opportunities that are surfacing.

Follow-through can be easily and appropriately done one-to-one by some team members. But remember that when follow-through is practiced by team members in two's, it permits them to support each other (the "with me" principle). In this way newer team members can be taught the skills of interpersonal relationships and can carry on the "team" approach to ministry.

When a team makes discussion about the people it serves a deliberate part of its meetings, it does so in a spirit of great humility. My friend Tom Saxon says, "Discernment is given for ministry — not for criticism or gossip." In other words, when a ministry team becomes aware of a person's needs and the opportunities for ministry to that person, that discernment is a gift from God meant for ministry, intended to build the person up. The goal of the team is to figure out what's happening in the lives of the people it serves and what specifically tailored response may be offered to each one that is appropriate for encouragement, faith development, and comfort.

It is *between* meetings that most of the follow-through assignments made during meetings are carried out. Suppose you're part of a group of thirty women who meet weekly to listen to a Bible teacher from nine to ten on Wednesday mornings. Immediately following, a dozen of the women go home after the teaching, and the rest of you separate into three small groups ("Word-Share-Prayer") that meet from 10:15 to 11:15. You're one of the small-group leaders, and as such you're on the ministry team along with the class teacher and the other small-group leaders. You meet every Friday from noon to one o'clock to consider the people-focus questions about the group:

Who was new last week?

Who was absent last week or has been absent for several weeks?

Who is hurting (because of illness, a family problem, or a work concern)?

Who appears open to joining a small group?

Who appears to be new to the Christian faith or interested in additional encouragement in discipleship?

You pray together about these questions in a spirit of humility: "Lord, help us understand the needs of the people you are bringing to us and the opportunities for ministry to them you are offering us, so that we may more effectively serve them." Suppose your team goes a step further: you determine who will follow through with each person you've talked about. "Mary, who is new this week, is a friend of mine," says Jenny, "so I'll follow through with her. I'll call her to tell her we're so glad she came and to invite her back. I'll also encourage her to join my small group." JoAnne, the team leader, says, "Judy is grieving the loss of her mother. Amy, you've experienced the loss of your mom. Would you take Laura with you and touch base with Judy?"

In this scenario, team members volunteer for follow-through assignments or accept suggestions made by the team leader or others on the team. They assess and address the needs of the people given to them. Follow-through ministry asks, "How may we be Christ's servant to each of these people?"

Now, in this illustration, after the women's study concluded, there were three small groups in which the women could grow more deeply in discipleship and friendship. If a woman in one of those groups was hurting or absent or indicating interest in additional spiritual growth, then the small-group leader and her leadership core would do the follow-through ministry. Still, the larger discussion of follow-through ensures the team isn't letting anyone fall through the cracks, especially those not in a small group.

Follow-through assignments are determined by who has the gift or heart or time to do them. If no one has the called-for "gift" for a particular ministry situation, then the team asks someone to act simply out of a serving heart, motivated out of love.

Follow-through assignments are also made based on the ministry responsibilities of team members. The person interested in joining a small group would be given to the team's small-group coordinator. If someone has indicated an interest in hospitality, then the person on the team concerned with making new people welcome would follow through, seeking to draw that person into the welcoming ministry.

As team members mature in offering ministry to others, they are to be increasingly encouraged to "love the many and focus on the few" — to encourage everyone in the ministry their team serves while engaging a few in personal ministry (as Jesus focused on the Twelve and on Mary, Martha, and Lazarus; as Paul focused on Timothy and Silvanus). In personal ministry we learn to give additional and intentional encouragement to others to grow spiritually by means of spiritual direction, small groups, and service with their spiritual gifts.

Of course, specific interpersonal follow-through makes little sense for task teams such as the sanctuary sound team or the parking-lot usher team, since they don't bear responsibility for identifying the visitor, the absent person, or the person in need. Nevertheless, every task-oriented ministry team can certainly covenant to have a prayer life on behalf of the people they're serving, even if they are unable to specifically name all of them. They can have a list of people who are considered potential team members for whom they pray on a daily basis. They can also agree to maintain the discipline of praying daily for specific people (for family, friends, and others in the church and community) so that even though their team's ministry is task-oriented, they are also involved in ministry to people through prayer.

Equipping Team Members for Interpersonal Ministry

Jesus sent the seventy-two out in two's. He sent two to get the colt for his triumphal entry on Palm Sunday, and he sent two to prepare the Upper Room. Team members can equip one another in interpersonal ministry by following this example, using the "with me" principle. The twosome is a "mini" ministry team. They pray together, they follow through together, they learn from each other, and they encourage each other. As the team matures, these "mini" teams may take people who aren't on the team along with them. As I've said before, genuine ministry skills are much more "caught" than "taught." Use seminars and workshops to teach the basics. Then use the "with me" principle to see them put into practice.

Engaging in Small-Group Life

The small-group experience — "Word-Share-Prayer" — is one of the most effective means of interpersonal ministry available to any team that is leading a group ministry. A small group is a caring fellowship and is the ultimate place of consistent, need-responsive ministry in the church. Like the four friends who carried their paralyzed companion to Jesus on a stretcher, group members stand by each other in times of difficulty. A small group is also a disciple-growing fellowship. Members grow in their knowledge of God and their understanding of Scripture. They also encourage each other to grow in their practice of the Christian lifestyle.

For these reasons, the ministry team organizes people into small-group Bible studies and affiliate ministry teams and sustains the small-group substructure within the overall group it leads. For groups of any size, the substructure of face-to-face small groups provides direct interpersonal ministry to every individual.

Whenever a team-led ministry is suitable to small-group formation, assign one person on the team the task of small-group coordinator. She will in turn lead an affiliate ministry team consisting of the leaders of the small groups. Small-group leaders may come from the larger group the team serves, although frequently those leaders will be members of the ministry team itself. The group the team serves now begins to have a growing subgroup structure — the leadership team itself, the affiliate ministry teams that carry out various tasks on behalf of the ministry team, and small groups. (For more information on small-group life, see the extensive section in Chapter Seven.)

Conclusion

Some teams are group leadership teams whose ministry includes both the task requirements of group life and the nurturing of those in the group. Such teams address the activity requirements of the group while simultaneously focusing on people before the group's meetings by praying for them and considering their needs, during the meetings by attending to and connecting people, and after the meetings in interpersonal follow-through. The group leadership team and its affiliate task-ministry teams plan their efforts after assessing the needs of the people they serve.

Some teams are task ministry teams that carry out specific responsibilities. While addressing their tasks they also engage in the double focus of ministry by considering the needs of the people they serve. The sanctuary sound team oversees the sound that worshippers hear, addressing their needs by asking, "Is the sound too loud, too soft? Is it audible everywhere in the room?" The kitchen team oversees everything from food preparation to kitchen cleanliness while asking, "Are the meals suitable to the dietary requirements, tastes, and budgets of our people?" Task-team members also carry out interpersonal ministry as they are equipped and sent to do so.

The practice of ministry is always the influence of "life on life" enabled by the ministry of the Holy Spirit. Ministry teams teach us, encourage us, help us, and thrust us into relationships with other people. We learn to trust God and to leave the results of our ministry to God.

CHAPTER TEN

Mobilizing the Team's Ministry of Program

The team's double focus of ministry includes people and program. Every ministry team has a particular work to do. Remember that the original meaning of "team" was the harnessing of two or more animals to pull a load. It is immediately obvious that every member of every team has a load to pull. When the members pull together, the team gets its work done.

In a recent capital stewardship campaign at my church, we assembled a team to lead the congregation in raising funds for a new multipurpose facility. Every task assignment — such as the home gatherings, the publicity materials, the arrangements for a congregational breakfast, and the children's activities — was matched with a person of appropriate passion, ability, and initiative. The program focus of the team clarifies the ministry team's vision and determines the roles, responsibilities, and work assignments for each member. First we develop plans, and then we send our people to accomplish those plans by God's grace.

Developing Plans

Undertaking Needs Assessment for People-Responsive Planning

The link between the people focus and the program focus of a ministry team is that the purpose of program is to serve people. As a matter of discipline, we always begin our planning efforts by considering the people who will be impacted by the team's ministry.

Some years ago, the congregation I serve began a ministry to men with a small group that met at six on Friday mornings. Then we added another group and another, until there were eleven small groups meeting every week. At that point we decided it was time to draw them together by inviting everyone on an overnight retreat. I asked six men to meet me for an early breakfast meeting at a local restaurant to plan the event. As we began to consider the issues to be solved, the immediate questions were all "pure task" in nature: "Who can we get to speak?" "Who will invite the speaker? "Who will get the refreshments?" "Who will set up the chairs and tables?" "Who will handle the publicity and registration?" After a few minutes of this, I said, "These questions address the needs of the program. Before we address any of these issues, let's think about the needs of the people so that what we do on the retreat serves the needs of these men as husbands, fathers, workers, retirees, believers, and seekers." Because we built a people focus into our planning process, the retreat was a great success, and men were encouraged in ways that were deeply significant to their spiritual and personal lives.

Many of us have been trained through traditional committee experiences to move as quickly as possible to task and program issues. As a result, a leadership team may be inclined to jump directly to its program focus — "What are we going to do next week, next month?" — without reviewing the needs of the people it serves. In order to sustain its people focus, the team resists the pressure to begin its planning by assessing the needs of the program. Instead, it assesses the needs of the people first and designs appropriate program response second. The team also engages in its people focus through interpersonal ministry and through organizing small groups. Consideration of people's needs and appropriate program response link people and program together in the double focus of ministry.

People are always the real subject of our ministry, whether we focus on them interpersonally or through task and program. The double focus of ministry helps a task-oriented ministry team to create a culture in which the team makes sure that its task serves people and is not an end in itself. Task teams that handle the program requirements of a group's meetings (facility set-up, publicity, greeting, music, sound system, and program) may also undertake significant interpersonal ministry. Once the meeting or event is underway, some of the task teams will continue to have purely programmatical responsibilities (for upfront speaking, the music, the sound system, and so on). Others will no longer have duties and will be free to focus on people, using the methods of interpersonal ministry described in the previous chapter.

Thinking Ahead

The word "amuse" is actually the combination of two words: "a," meaning "not," and "muse," meaning "think." We dwell in an age of amusement, a "not-thinking" age in which a variety of experiences occupy our attention, often diminishing our interest or opportunity to simply think about what we're doing. We are also living in the age of busyness, which further reduces the time we have to think. Yet vital and effective leaders think ahead and think clearly about vision: where they're going and what they're going to do about it now.

Many of us live under intense time pressure, and we tend to move from event to event without much forethought. In such busy times, thinking ahead and planning must become spiritual disciplines, as significant for the development of a ministry as the more traditional spiritual disciplines of prayer and Bible study. We use our "minds of Christ" and ask the Spirit to lead our planning. To make planning a spiritual discipline practiced by the team, the leader and leadership core determine a "thinking ahead" rhythm that will work for the team, such as one that involves an annual or semi-annual reflective process and a simple monthly review process.

Think about your team vision: where you're going, and what needs to be done next. The very process of thinking through where you are and where you want to go will help keep the team on task and align or re-align team members with roles that will be the most fruitful. The more frequently the team thinks about these things, the more responsive it will be to changing issues and opportunities in the culture in which it ministers.

Washington Irving once said, "Great minds have purposes; others have wishes." A vision without a plan is only a wish. Thinking ahead puts wheels on our vision, attaches actions, timelines, and deadlines to them. Plans become the hinge between our dreams and our reality. Vision defines where we want to go; thinking ahead shows us how to get there. The necessity for sound thinking increases with the complexity and significance of the vision to be accomplished. Nevertheless, thinking ahead is easily sidestepped in our activity-driven culture.

Thinking ahead can appear to be non-productive. After all, we aren't *doing* anything. We're merely thinking! And thinking ahead can be a hassle, especially for those of us in the "do-it" generation (preferring action over thought) or the "view-it" generation (perferring entertainment of all kinds). But we need to resist this way of looking at things. We must make thinking about our team's life and vision and activities a spiritual discipline because God works through the process of prayerful, reflective thought to give us wisdom for our team's work. On a consistent and ongoing basis we must ask for God's guidance. "If any of you lacks wisdom, he should ask God, who gives generously to all without finding fault, and it will be given to him" (James 1:5).

Two extremes are inadequate forethought and too much forethought. With too little forethought, which is increasingly common in our over-busy age, key opportunities can be missed, critical problems ignored. A practical solution to the problem of inadequate forethought is having the team decide how it will abide by the covenantal agreement known as "Clear Expectations." Make this a matter of the team's annual calendar. Once or twice a year, schedule a time of major review and fresh planning. Then refine such thinking with monthly reviews and weekly updates. If your team is in a highly pressured environment, it may not be able to take much time out solely for thinking ahead. If this is the case, find a way to practice "thinking ahead on the run," building the thinking time right into your regular meetings. Whatever you do, don't give up on this. The old adage "If you fail to plan, you plan to fail" is still quite true for any vision of great complexity, significance, and difficulty.

On the other hand, some of us devote too much time to thinking ahead. We try to discern all of the issues in exhaustive detail, set complex goals, and devise intricate solutions to potential challenges. We might be filling a lot of paper, but all too frequently we're taking no action — in fact, we're weighed down with too much detail. Spontaneity and the freedom to react to changing circumstances and opportunities are things we want to keep at the same time we think ahead.

The team leader may lead the thinking-ahead process, but this isn't a requirement, especially if there are others on the team with a facility for this. What is essential is that the leader and leadership core ensure that thinking ahead is as much a part of the overall life of the team as its small-group life and its ministry activities.

Sustaining and Advancing Vision

When I was a child, sometimes my gym teachers would have me and the other kids run in place. We exerted considerable energy without going anywhere! Without an effective planning process, our tendency is to abandon the consideration of our purposes as a congregation and the needs of the people we seek to serve and simply figure out the same old "program mechanics": speakers, refreshments, and publicity.

I have come to call this the "Law of Programmatic Inertia." Programs set in motion tend to continue in their original pattern until acted on by some external force. The result? We run in place. Of course, this makes for both stability and vulnerability. Stability in a sound ministry, like a spring of water, can bring ongoing refreshment into people's lives year after year. On the other hand, programs repeated year after year are vulnerable to growing stale and out of step with people's current needs.

Some years ago, two Harvard Business School professors, Robert H. Hayes and William J. Abernathy, made a remarkable observation.[1] They contended that the crisis in American business at the time was rooted in the preference of American managers to service existing markets, to imitate rather than to innovate, and to aim at short-term returns. We in the church often think the same way, maintaining the programs and ministries we already have. We keep running in place.

A particularly useful way for a ministry team to think of vision is in terms of *sustaining* and *advancing* vision.[2] To sustain a work is to con-

---

1. Robert H. Hayes and William J. Abernathy, "Managing Our Way to Economic Decline," *Harvard Business Review* 58 (July/August 1980): 67-77.

2. This is the third shift in my book entitled *Twelve Dynamic Shifts for Transforming Your Church* (Grand Rapids: Eerdmans, 2002).

tinue to increase its effectiveness. There's nothing wrong with running last year's program over again if that program is indeed accomplishing the team's vision. Sustaining vision doesn't mean developing a new vision, but it does require deliberate planning to maintain the impact and quality of the work being done to implement the vision. Advancing vision pushes the team to consider new ways to improve its effectiveness. Advancing vision may expand the scope of the team's activities. It may increase the excellence and quality of what's already being done.

It is much easier for some of us to tinker with existing programs than to generate the vision, leadership, and resources needed for new endeavors. But if sustaining and advancing aren't part of the vision of our team, we've consigned ourselves to a purely maintaining vision. When that occurs, our current level of performance dictates what our future actions will be. Before long we run the risk of running in place again.

Effective ministry-team leadership in long-established ministries holds sustaining and advancing vision in critical balance. Not 50-50, but more like 90-10 — giving 90 percent of the effort to sustaining what is and 10 percent to advancing what can be. The 90-10 pattern permits us to ensure adequate stability of the work while we advance simultaneously in scope and excellence. Of course, a new endeavor will reverse the numbers, with 90 percent of the effort put into getting things going!

Advancing vision can mean there will be more and more to sustain. As the scope and amount of team activity grow, new people must be involved. Otherwise, the available time and energy of the existing members will limit what they can accomplish so that no significant advancing vision can be implemented. Again, the team will run in place. With advancing vision, team members develop progressively from "doers of ministry" to leaders of doers as they lead their own affiliate teams.

Employing the Action Learning Process

With the advent of the concept of the "learning organization," as described by Peter Senge in his book entitled *The Fifth Discipline,* many of us in congregational ministry have realized that long-established congregations generally have not been learning organizations.[3] The tendency has been to rely on the same basic approach to ministry despite massive changes going on in the world around us.

Robert L. Dilworthy, associate professor of adult education at Virginia Commonwealth University, remarks, "Change now tends to outdistance our ability to learn. Established knowledge can quickly be outdistanced by the pace of new challenges and events. . . . Knowledge on hand [existing knowledge] tends to misdirect inquiry rather than facilitate problem resolution."[4] In other words, what we know can mislead us. Think about that! The ways we have practiced ministry in the past may no longer be effective today. In these times of turbulent, high-velocity change, the church that merely repeats its past ministries over again will be increasingly out of touch with what it takes to reach people in today's world. Michael Marquardt, professor of human resources development at George Washington University, contends, "People and organizations need to learn new ways of coping with problems. Only by improving the learning capacity of individuals and organizations can we deal with the dynamics of change."[5] Ministry teams are one of the powerful ways that a church may become a "learning congregation," because the teams will seek the new understandings and insights necessary to move forward.

One of the most useful approaches to learning and leadership presently available is what is known as "action learning," a subject about which Marquardt has written a book. Action learning combines a commitment to action with a commitment to learning. Action learning is a problem-solving process used in organizations around the world to inspire fresh learning, decisive action, and team-life development. It has been shown to contribute to the esprit de corps and the vision of the entire organization. Action learning can enable a congregation to become a learning organization that shows

3. Peter Senge, *The Fifth Discipline* (New York: Doubleday, 1990).

4. Robert L. Dilworth, "Action Learning in a Nutshell," *Performance Improvement Quarterly* 11, no. 1 (1988): 34.

5. Michael J. Marquardt, *Action Learning in Action: Transforming Problems and People for World-Class Organizational Learning* (Palo Alto, Calif.: Davies-Black Publishing, 1999), p. 22.

honor to its past while it embraces the new ideas and practices necessary for it to remain on the cutting edge of reaching, growing, and sending people.

As Marquardt explains, action learning enables problem solving, organizational learning, team building, leadership development, and personal development.[6] The power of the action learning concept is that it permits a group within your congregation to become contagiously excited about addressing an aspect of the congregation's defining vision or tackling a major opportunity or obstacle/problem, to think originally about it, to learn new ways to address it, and to conclude with very concrete action — which itself contributes to learning.

Marquardt identifies six key elements of the action learning process: the project question, the action learning team, the questioning and reflection process, the commitment to learning, the facilitator, and the resolution to take action.[7] The ministry team may employ each of these six elements whenever it has a complex issue to address.

The Project Question: This may be an objective (goal), such as fulfilling the team's defining vision; an opportunity, such as beginning a new ministry to blended families; or an obstacle the team would like to address, such as how to attract younger members.

The Action Learning Team: This involves a diverse group of four to eight capable, imaginative people who are interested in the project question. A larger ministry team can use subgroups of the team to tackle a complex issue.

The Questioning and Reflection Process: This process emphasizes asking the right questions rather than giving the right answers so that learning the new is as significant as stating what we already know. In this process, people first ask questions to clarify the nature of the problem, and then during a period of reflection identify possible solutions in a nondefensive environment. When working on the issue at hand, team members are reminded to ask questions rather than just speaking about what they think or know. It is this questioning process that generates new insights. Every team member comes to the meetings with questions for the whole group to consider.

---

6. Marquardt, *Action Learning in Action,* p. 5.

7. Marquardt, *Action Learning in Action,* pp. 6-8.

The Commitment to Learning: The learning is as important as the action. Action learning places equal emphasis on problem-solving and organizational and personal development. In other words, instead of merely brainstorming about solutions to a problem using already known information, the team aggressively seeks new information and new insights using the questioning/reflecting process in order to discover the best possible means of addressing a complex issue.

The Facilitator (Learning Coach): A learning coach is designated to keep the focus on learning as well as action and guides the team to reflect on both its learning and its problem-solving. The learning coach is not the ministry-team leader and is not as concerned with the details of how the group is deciding what to do as with whether or not the group is learning as it is problem-solving. This is important because we often want to jump to the "who will do what" stage immediately, and thus we can wind up skipping all the important learning that enables our team and our congregation to move from maintenance to innovation in ministry and mission. The learning coach ensures that adequate reflection occurs before action is taken.

The learning coach ensures that everyone has the opportunity to ask questions and to speak freely. When the team is engaged in specific discussion, the coach has the authority, when necessary, to "neutralize with grace" anyone who might squelch conversation in a particular direction, so that a full conversation can take place. After all alternatives are on the table, issues are addressed that ensure that the action the team ultimately takes is consistent with the defining vision and practices or concerns of its congregation or ministry.

The Resolution to Take Action: Real learning comes with action. The action learning team takes action. Its goal isn't to submit a report to congregational leaders asking if the team can act on its findings. The team seeks upfront permission to carry out its plan with the support of the governing body — assuming, of course, that the plan shows adequate preparation and is consistent with the defining vision of the congregation. The team keeps congregational leaders informed of its progress and plans so there are no surprises for them and there is continuing support from them.

Sending People

Determining Roles and Responsibilities

There are a great many ways to organize a team to accomplish its vision. Creative people will work with the level of initiative, abilities, and experience of the team members so that every one of them assumes some responsibility in the fulfillment of the team vision and engages in interpersonal ministry as is appropriate. Excellent resources are available to assist the mobilization of a team in the accomplishment of its work.[8] Most of the material on teams published in management circles as well as for the church focuses on the important matters surrounding task and role definition: who is going to do what and getting the right people connected to the right responsibilities. In using such resources we bear in mind that a ministry team ensures that the tasks related to its own growth in discipleship and fellowship are appropriately covered as well as the tasks associated with the team's organizing vision.

Team members ask for or accept responsibilities preferably based on their spiritual gifts and interests, but always based on a willingness to serve. People often join teams because they have an interest in the team's purpose or want to work with a particular team leader, without having a clear idea of what their task assignment is going to be. Their individual assignments are worked out as their gifts and abilities are matched with the team's current needs. If the team needs more people to accomplish its work, it begins the process of identifying and inviting new members. Once a team has been in operation for a while, it will simultaneously conceive of roles and invite people to join the team to fulfill them, *and* it will adapt the present roles of team members to make better make use of their initiative, abilities, and experience.

The process of determining the tasks necessary and the abilities required for their accomplishment is similar to the process by which

---

8. A good web site on teams is http://www.workteams.unt.edu. See also Ken Blanchard, Donald Carew, and Eunice Parisi-Carew, *The One-Minute Manager Builds High-Performing Teams* (New York: William Morrow, 2000), and Stephen L. Schey and Walt Kallestad, *Team Ministry* (Nashville: Abingdon Press, 1996).

committees assign work to committee members. In the task orientation of a team, every person plays a key role.

Basic to team-member assignments are the biblical teachings concerning the ministry (priesthood) of every believer, spiritual giftedness, and a serving heart. If a congregation has a ministry mobilization team that systematically assesses each congregational participant's spiritual gifts and interests in ministry, then the "placement" of people of ability and congruent vision on appropriate teams is greatly enhanced.[8]

Each role fulfills part of the team's vision. Some people may wear more than one hat. Team members may in turn lead affiliate ministry teams to help accomplish their assigned task. Teams periodically adjust task assignments according to who carries out their work promptly and who puts it off, who has gifts and abilities not recognized at the outset, and which team members want to try different assignments because of changing interests. Good team leaders know that they need to carry their fair share of the work, following through with team members, reminding them of deadlines and raising issues as necessary, and encouraging them.

There are a variety of ways in which team members may be given their individual responsibilities. The team leader may function like a committee chairperson who assigns each person a task (or who recognizes who has volunteered for what). Then there is the team with a person other than the leader whose role is to help each member discover his or her role. Other team assignments come out of dialog among the team members as they discern together who might best do what and who wants to do what; then they hold each other accountable for accomplishing the assignments.

In her excellent book entitled *Volunteers: How to Get Them, How to Keep Them*, Helen Little details twelve needs of every volunteer who is asked to assume a role:

1. A specific, manageable task with a beginning and an end.
2. A task that matches interests and reasons for volunteering.
3. A good reason for doing the task.
4. Written instructions.

9. See Sue Mallory, *The Equipping Church* (Grand Rapids: Zondervan, 2001).

5. A reasonable deadline for completing the task.
6. Freedom to complete the task *when* and *where* it is most convenient for the volunteer.
7. Everything necessary to complete the task without interruption.
8. Adequate training.
9. A safe, comfortable, and friendly working environment.
10. Follow-up to see that the task is completed.
11. An opportunity to provide feedback when the task is finished.
12. Appreciation, recognition, and rewards that match the reasons for volunteering.[10]

These are all good ideas for shaping the tasks of ministry-team members.

As a member of a ministry team, I would summarize my overall role this way:

To serve Christ by growing in personal discipleship
- Through the practice of spiritual disciplines such as daily devotions
- Through prayer partnerships with other team members

To serve Christ by building the fellowship of the ministry team
- Through my team's small-group life and shared meals
- Through time spent with other team members in life and leisure to nurture friendships

To serve Christ by focusing on the people in the ministry my team leads
- Through regularly praying for the people by name
- Through spontaneous and/or intentional acts of interpersonal follow-through using the six defining practices of fostering discipleship

To serve Christ by accomplishing specific works or tasks
- Through the use of my spiritual gifts and a serving heart
- Through bringing all the initiative, abilities, and experience I have to bear on these tasks

---

10. Helen Little, *Volunteers: How to Get Them, How to Keep Them* (Nashville: Panacea Press, 1999), p. 19.

Sending Team Members to Ministry

"Sending," one of the six defining practices of transformational ministry, is the practice of connecting team members to specific ministry through interpersonal and task assignments in accord with their spiritual gifts and interests. We have "sending" in mind from the moment we first invite an individual onto the team. In this way we follow Jesus' example, who appointed the Twelve and then sent them to ministry. The very word "apostle" means "sent one." The Twelve understood that their destiny was to be sent from the first moment Jesus invited them to be with him.

Sending doesn't mean that a person leaves the team. Sending means that she accepts responsibility for a particular assignment and is "sent" to do it. This not only develops discipleship in the team member; it also enables the team to fulfill its vision. Sending is the key to mobilizing every team member for ministry, expanding the scope of the team's ministry, and increasing the number of people engaged in the work of the team. Linking a person to a task that draws on her area of passion and interest as well as her willingness to serve, her spiritual gifts, her experiences, and her abilities is a critical facet of sending each individual to the right ministry. (For a more detailed explanation, see Chapter Six.)

Understanding the True Nature of Sending

I want to devote additional attention to the concept of sending because this isn't a practice that we do particularly well today, either as the formal process of delegation within a hierarchical organization or as the process by which a decentralized ministry team empowers both individuals and teams to act. Connecting people to ministry is not the sole responsibility of the pastor, congregational leaders, or the ministry mobilization team. It is the responsibility of every ministry team — indeed, of every believer.

Sending Is Deeper than Delegating

The Latin word meaning "to send" is *legare*. Interestingly, *legare* is the root of the English word *delegate*. To delegate is to entrust a responsibility or opportunity for service to someone. It is to give someone the authority to act. To delegate is to hand a portion of the team's vision over to a person or another team to accomplish. In that sense, when a team leader delegates or entrusts a task to a team member, that person has been "sent" to ministry.

Yet "sending" has another, deeper meaning. Recall how Paul and Barnabas were "sent" by the church in Antioch with the defining vision and practices of that church embedded in their own lives, yet they were completely free to act as they saw fit on their missionary journey (Acts 13). Sending is more than giving people a task. It is releasing them to pursue the vision as they understand God is calling them to accomplish it. In sending we offer prayers and encouragement as a person or a team undertakes a particular ministry endeavor.

Sending is the biblical word for our practice of trusting a team member or an entire team to pursue a ministry vision. There are instructive examples of sending in both the Old and New Testaments:

- Moses' father-in-law replied, "What you are doing is not good. You and these people who come to you will only wear yourselves out. . . . But select capable men from all the people — men who fear God, trustworthy men who hate dishonest gain — and appoint them as officials. . . ." (Exod. 18:17, 21a)
- He appointed twelve — designating them apostles — that they might be with him and that he might send them out to preach. (Mark 3:14)
- Again Jesus said, "Peace be with you! As the Father has sent me, I am sending you." (John 20:21)
- So when we could stand it no longer, we thought it best to be left by ourselves in Athens. We sent Timothy, who is our brother and God's fellow worker in spreading the gospel of Christ, to strengthen and encourage you in your faith. (1 Thess. 3:1-2)

Sending Requires Equipping for Ministry

To ready a team member for sending, assess her spiritual gifts and abilities but stop with assessment. Then connect her to deliberate and thorough training that will further develop her gifts and prepare her for the assignment she will be carrying out. This may involve apprenticing her with someone already doing the task she is being prepared for and offering sound coaching.

Equipping for ministry includes both teaching and training. Teaching focuses on information; training focuses on skill development. Teaching focuses on knowing; training focuses on know-how. Equipping means imparting the information the team member needs as well as supplying the actual experience she needs to apply what she is learning.

Taking these steps also works to build a person's relationship with Jesus Christ. He is the ultimate equipper of those in ministry and will continue to equip your team members for ministry for the rest of their lives.

Sending Is Permission-Giving

In an earlier chapter we reviewed the six levels of sending, beginning with the very tight directive of "Do what we ask you to do." At times we ask a person to undertake a specific assignment on behalf of the team. In order to develop people of vision and initiative, our goal is to move in the direction of the looser levels of sending, which say, "Act on your own." This gives people the permission and blessing to pursue their own vision for ministry within the context of the overall ministry of the team.

In the congregation I serve, Pam Volk expressed her concern for the unemployed. The idea for her ministry was not in the "plans" of church leaders; no conversation about the unemployed had been a part of their thinking ahead about the congregation. Still, they recognized that such a ministry would address a significant need in the lives of several church members, so they blessed and "sent" Pam to develop a special ministry called "Unemployment Anonymous" that has connected several seekers with employment.

Jayme Bauer, Jean Crane, Mike Holohan, and Marla Kemmler developed a passion to refurbish and redecorate the entryways of our church building to make them more inviting and hospitable than the "institutional" look we had had for years. They also wanted to make the church more inviting by explaining the ministry opportunities of the congregation to those walking in the door. That wasn't a particular passion of those responsible for facility maintenance at the time, but the new team was "sent" and given permission to pursue their dreams, and the results have been dramatic and effective.

Sending Multiplies Ministry

Sending multiplies the ministry of the team. Obviously there is a limit to what you can do by yourself. No matter how gifted and able you may be, there's a limit to the number of details you can track, a limit to the number of people you can relate to personally and directly supervise. When you and your team have greater vision to undertake other projects or expand the scope of the team's present ministry, then sending is the key to enjoining others to help you accomplish the vision.

Sending Is Not a Solo Act

Since team-based ministry is relational "with me" ministry, when we send any given person to ministry, we also work with that person to discern with whom they will serve. It might be with one other person on a "mini-team," following Jesus' example of sending people in two's, or with a larger ministry team, depending on what the task demands. We don't send someone to a task alone unless the particular ministry assignment requires it.

Sending with Effectiveness

Avoiding Hindrances to Sending

So why are there so few excellent "senders" — delegaters in the church? I believe there are a number of contributing factors.

- *Mindset:* We simply don't think in terms of sending people. We think of ministry as caring for individuals or teaching groups or handling a task assignment by ourselves. Sending means carefully and intentionally thinking about how to get others with us in ministry and then deploying them to fulfill their own emerging visions for ministry.
- *Pride:* This is the "I can do it better than anyone else" problem. We like the limelight. But sending means letting go, in all humility, of some things others have praised us for. There is a basic arrogance underlying the notion that "I am the *only one* who can do it right." While it may be true that you are the best at a particular task, or maybe the only one who can currently do it, you have to realize that you can't increase your own effectiveness unless you equip others to do what you're doing and send them to do it. Sending means accepting the possibility that the task won't be done the way you would do it. Sending also means giving others the opportunity for fruitful and life-fulfilling service, and recognizing that the credit for that service will go to them.

   In the book entitled *Leading and Managing Your Church,* Bob Logan describes a seminar he once gave on delegation. One pastor raised his hand and asked, "What if everything you're doing is something only you can do?" Bob responded, "I would find it highly unusual if someone was so omnicompetent that absolutely nothing could be delegated to someone else. Perhaps you're the exception." The next day Bob went out to lunch with this pastor and discovered that he typed the bulletin and ordered the office supplies, two tasks that Bob had mentioned the day before as examples of things that pastors could delegate. When Bob asked the pastor why he typed the bulletin, the pastor answered, "That's easy. I'm the fastest typist in the church." Bob then asked, "Do you have anyone in your church who could type the bulletin with the level of quality that you need?" The pastor thought for a moment and said, "Yes, there is one woman — but she only types forty words a minute." At this point Bob thought, *I'd better go slowly here*. Gradually Bob helped the pastor see that he was robbing the woman of an opportunity to serve Christ and that the time she saved him could be devoted to things only he could do.[11]

- *Laziness:* Sending is work! Vital congregations have far more activity happening than can be conducted by the pastoral staff alone. To send, we must invite someone to the task, equip him to do it, and send him. We often don't do it simply because it takes extra effort. It's inconvenient, yes — but well worth it.

- *Fear:* We fear losing control over the task or the ministry area. For those accustomed to hierarchical "top-down" leadership that expects to be asked for permission and is used to higher levels of control, the idea of "letting people go" can lead to some anxiety. The more freedom we give people to initiate, the less we have to say about what they do. Sending means placing decisions, responsibility, and opportunity into the hands of others. We fear they might botch the job and leave us "holding the bag."

We might also be afraid to ask others to do something because we picture them resisting or complaining or just saying no. We are anxious at the prospect of asking a busy or intimidating person to take on a particular responsibility. We need to remember to call on godly courage, the will to act that comes from faith in Jesus Christ. We need to recall the Scripture text that encourages us to be strong, be of good courage, and do it. Let God's people go!

Sending Progressively

The "send" step is usually best practiced by degrees. I find it helpful to think in terms of progressive sending. The person is initially asked to apprentice with someone else doing the task. As she develops in com-

11. Carl F. George and Robert E. Logan, *Leading and Managing Your Church* (Old Tappan, N.J.: Revell, 1987), p. 118.

petence and wisdom, her level of responsibility is increased. Eventually the team leader and leadership core send her with all of the freedom appropriate to her initiative, abilities, and experience.

Encouraging the "Sent One" with Scheduled Times for Ministry Review and Thinking Ahead

Inherent in the practice of sending, of deploying team members in ministry, is a review of their work. Ministry review considers what has been accomplished. With highly competent team members who have experience and initiative, little review will be necessary other than to offer praise to God and to them for their work. With less able, less experienced, or less self-directed team members, a higher level of support may be needed to enable them to follow through.

At stake are the matters of accountability and encouragement. The highly motivated person is intrinsically motivated and holds herself accountable *to herself* to accomplish the work. Your encouragement will affirm her, but the fact is that she will drive herself. The individual who is less motivated or in some ways less capable will need greater support if he is to accomplish his work well and in a timely manner. He is extrinsically motivated, and encouragement helps him function at his best.

As Elizabeth O'Connor eloquently wrote, "How does another person know that we have taken what he has said with any seriousness if we do not ask what he has done with his gift? The reason our groups go through the process of naming our gifts and making explicit our covenant is so that we can grow in responsibility and move toward authentic freedom. The person who is seriously interested in investing his life does not perceive the time of accounting as something to be anticipated with dread, but as a caring which supports and encourages him in what he wants to do."[12]

As the quotation from O'Connor suggests, this is not a "performance" review in which a person is measured against objective standards with accompanying compensation or penalty. It's a positive time

---

12. Elizabeth O'Connor, *The Eighth Day of Creation* (Waco, Tex.: Word Books, 1971), pp. 32-33.

of reflection, support, encouragement, and the consideration of next steps in relation to vision and goals.

Some reviews and times of thinking ahead are informal and brief. You might see a teammate at the water fountain or take a moment to phone her. You ask how things are going and offer a simple word of counsel and encouragement. If there's a problem with her work, don't "save up" your concerns. Follow up immediately with a conversation in which you address any difficulties. This is a time to forego e-mail and talk face-to-face or on the phone.

Other reviews are more formal and scheduled regularly. A useful technique in leading those who have assumed responsibilities on a team is to schedule monthly or quarterly times for ministry review and thinking ahead. Such reviews may be conducted on a one-to-one basis or as a group discussion among the team. For team members who carry significant responsibility, personal reviews between the team member and the team leader may be preferable.

When meeting one to one, remember that the purpose of the conversation is to move forward. Build up the team member. Ask him how he's doing. Communicate respect, interest, appreciation, and encouragement. Review his ministry. Focus on people: Who is with you? How are they doing? How are you developing them? And focus on accomplishment: What has happened? What have you done? Then look ahead: What is your vision? What are the next steps, with whom will you take them, and what support do you need to accomplish them? Finally, pray. Thank God for the blessings and accomplishments given and look forward to the steps ahead.

Conclusion

The team fulfills the vision for which it is organized as it develops plans, using processes like action learning to address complex issues. It deploys its members to the tasks identified in its planning by deliberately "sending" its members to ministry, scheduling regular times of review and thinking ahead, and practicing the essentials of sound leadership. The result is a highly effective team capable of responding to complex issues and of accomplishing great vision by the grace of God.

Get Changed, Get Together, and Get Going!

Sam Shoemaker, the great Episcopalian pastor and co-founder of Alcoholics Anonymous, used to say over and over, "Get changed, get together, and get going." Good advice then, and good advice now. My friend Dick Meyer suggests a change in the order of the phrasing: "Get together, get changed, and get going." Teams begin by getting together. As they seek their Lord, they are changed. As they embrace their ministry, they get going.

Begin a team-based ministry. Get together with those who will join you in fulfilling a vision for ministry or with those with whom you are already engaged in ministry. Begin small-group life together, and then get changed. Seek God's vision for your own lives and for your ministry. Establish some additional practices to develop your friendships, such as the shared meal, the prayer covenant, and the overnight retreat. Then get going. Be strong, be of good courage, and do it!

Introducing ministry-team practices to a newly forming team can be a truly exciting experience as people of passion for a mission come to discover the team itself will be an instrument of God in their own growth in faith and friendship. Take care to implement these practices in the very first meetings of a new team. If a new team begins by focusing solely on its mission without paying deliberate attention to its small-group life and other covenantal agreements, then it quickly becomes a committee in practice and a ministry team in name only.

If you're going to introduce the team concept into a traditional congregation with a long history of committee-based leadership, it will require clarity of vision on the part of the pastor and other senior leaders and opinion-makers in the life of the church. Typically those using committee approaches to getting work done have never used any other approach. They may be nervous about the prospect of giving teams a greater degree of autonomy, even though such teams faithfully center themselves on the defining vision and practices of the congregation. Clarity of vision will help people realize that in moving to a ministry-team approach they aren't giving up the strengths of the committee concept but are adding the encouraging dimensions of discipleship and friendship.

Making the change will also require a long-term commitment. Old habits have a remarkable way of slowing a congregation's shift from traditional to transformational practices. Congregations can be like rubber bands. You can pull and push a rubber band into any shape you want, but when you let go, it snaps back into its original configuration. Only long-term commitment to the process of transition can assure the consistency of vision that ultimately will permanently reshape the congregation's approach to leadership and ministry.

Think about the nature of transition. One way to try to make team ministry a defining practice of a congregation would involve requiring that every current committee shift to the ministry-team format imme-diately and that every new ministry begin only when a team is in place. But this kind of imposition of change usually results in resistance from existing committees and many key leaders. A better way of bringing about this change involves making team life a defining practice into which the congregation will be gracefully led over two or more years. To do this, train your leaders in ministry-team life. Bless those who aren't ready for team life, and work with those who are, giving them ongoing support and counsel. When a new ministry is conceived, seek leaders who embrace the ministry-team vision as well as the vision for the new ministry. Think in terms of sustaining vision and advancing vision. As you recall, sustaining vision maintains with excellence those ministries that already exist in your congregation, while advancing vision involves developing those new ministry approaches and endeavors that bring transformation into the congregation's life.

Lift up your ministry-team leaders and teams before the congrega-tion. Give public recognition to their work as a means of honoring them and modeling the way for others.

Gather a few people around you to make a "ministry team" ministry team with whom you study this material and think through the next steps you will take. If necessary, speak to key decision-makers and opinion-makers personally to get their support. It may require considerable effort to lead a congregation to change committees to teams and to move from higher levels of "control" at the board level to higher levels of permission-giving "sending" ministries. But the result is certainly worth it: empowered people growing as disciples and pursuing ministry vision with passion — and a transformational congregation.

In making this transition — as with any transition in the life of the congregation — be prayerful. Ask God for clarity of vision and for guidance in leading others to the ministry-team process and in discerning whom to invite onto your ministry teams.

Clearly, the essence of ministry-team life is living life together and learning to trust and serve God together. As we read in First John, "We proclaim to you what we have seen and heard, so that you also may have fellowship with us. And our fellowship is with the Father and with his Son, Jesus Christ" (1:3). In team life we emphasize growth in discipleship and fellowship and are guided by the double focus of ministry on people and task accomplishment. In team life we learn to believe that God is working in each of us and through us together. We learn to believe that this is *God's* ministry, and that we are an extension of God's love to those people whom the team serves.

No wonder there is great power in ministry teams. God has great plans for your congregation and for your ministry team. Believe it and move out in God's grace and power!

Ministry-Team Covenants and Courtesies

1. We are deliberate about our relationships and fellowship, honoring the covenantal agreements known as the Seven Threads of Ministry-Team Relationships:

Spiritual Disciplines: Our team engages in the disciplines of the Christian faith such as worship, prayer, and Bible study (together and alone), fellowship, and ministry. We pray daily for our ministry and for each other by name.

Face-to-Face Relationships: We work to know one another on a personal basis, to trust and serve one another. We work out our differences with mutual respect and love.

Confidentiality: We keep team conversation within the team. We respect the confidences of others.

Communication: We communicate directly and thoroughly. We introduce significant issues face-to-face. We use voice mail and e-mail to communicate information and affirmation but never confrontation. We resolve differences in person or on the phone. We avoid indirect communication, with the exception of passing along praise and compliments to one another.

Clear Expectations: We clarify and understand our common vision. We establish communal and individual expectations, and we communicate clearly what we intend to accomplish and when. We use weekly, monthly, and yearly conversations with the team and with the team leader to guide us.

Loose-Tight Balance: We serve with freedom and within boundaries. The team blesses our initiative (loose) while we remain committed to the defining vision and practices of the team and of our congregation (tight).

Loving Loyalty: We have the freedom to express differences of opinion within the team while supporting team decisions to those outside the team.

2. We reflect the humility of Jesus Christ.

Our attitude is to be the same as that of Christ Jesus, "who, being in very nature God, did not consider equality with God something to be grasped" (Phil. 2:5-6).

The ministry of the whole body and the ministry of its parts are of equal value. We work simultaneously within the same body of believers, though with different responsibilities and in different ways. We do not subscribe to "turf pride," the idea that "my ministry is the most important." (See 1 Cor. 12:12-26.)

The various ministry teams such as the pastoral and program staff, the elders and deacons, the support staff, and the congregational ministry teams are parts of *one* overall congregational leadership team — all of equal value and significance. The seven covenantal agreements apply among the various ministry teams as well as within them.

"We are servants of the servants of the Servant," to use a phrase by Richard C. Halverson.

We represent Jesus Christ to the people we serve. "Follow my example," Paul said, "as I follow the example of Christ" (1 Cor. 11:1).

3. We observe important courtesies and guidelines.

- We respect congregational leadership. We center our team ministry on the defining vision and practices of our congregation.
- We recognize that time is as precious for others as it is for us. We begin and end our meetings on time, and we don't overtax someone's time with too large or complex an assignment.

- We keep our promises, commitments, appointments, and agreements.
- Our word is our bond.
- We use the "Good Report" principle, always speaking well of one another.
- If we are bothered by something happening on our team, we don't complain about it to our friends. Instead we go directly to the source and seek to work it out.
- When we make a mistake — or even if we don't, but discover that others are ill at ease with something we have done — we seek immediate reconciliation/restoration, and do so face-to-face if possible. (See Matt. 5:23-24.)
- We seek to generate vision with those whom we lead. Where appropriate and possible, we think ahead one year — or two or three years ahead when circumstances permit.
- We send every willing person to specific ministry.
- We begin new ministries only when there is a team in place.

Formats for the Ministry-Team Meeting

When to Meet

This is no small issue if your people are extremely busy or if they have particular schedule constraints. Schedule the meeting to allow the team to meet in its small-group format for at least twenty minutes before moving on to its personal and programmatic ministry issues. Schedule regular times to share a meal together, at least once every three months. One way to do that is to schedule a meeting and a meal together. Meet in the back room of an inexpensive restaurant or simply bring sack lunches with you. Some teams may prefer to meet regularly during a mealtime in order to enjoy the fellowship of a shared meal and accomplish their work as a team without having to schedule additional meetings.

Schedule considerations begin with the lifestyle and life-stage demands of the team members involved. For example, if a ministry to mothers of pre-schoolers occurs at nine-thirty on a weekday morning, the team could choose to meet for that hour directly before the gathering so that only one set of child-care arrangements would have to be made.

How Often to Meet

The classic church committee typically meets monthly for an hour or two to process its work. But since the ministry team seeks to accomplish its vision as well as sustain a significant level of initiative and develop a deep and ongoing experience of personal friendship and fellowship, it will have to meet more frequently than that.

If your team ministers to a group, one rule of thumb to consider is this: have the team meet as often as the group it leads. If the youth group meets every week, the youth ministry team meets every week or at least touches base long enough to decide what interpersonal follow-through actions to take. If the retired men's luncheon is held twice a month, the ministry team supporting it would meet at least twice a month.

For task ministry teams engaged in the accomplishment of specific work, the amount accomplished is also directly related to meeting frequency. For example, a team of small-group coaches may meet the first and third Tuesday evenings of each month, leaving them the second and fourth Tuesday evenings to meet with the small-group leaders. This commitment allows the coaches to sustain their own fellowship and ministry while accomplishing the task of coaching others.

Sample Ministry-Team Schedules

The sample schedules given below allow a team to cover a great deal of ground in a short length of time. Everyone on the team should know the schedule for the meeting and help each other stick to it. There is an obvious exception: Forego the agenda when someone on the team is clearly in the middle of a difficult situation. Minister to that person first and attend to other matters second.

A team's schedule should include the three major team concerns: "Word-Share-Prayer," people focus, and program focus. All three can be covered if the leader of the meeting pays attention to the time and if the team members are alert to the agenda. In regularly setting aside a short time for "Word-Share-Prayer," the team greatly enriches its experience of fellowship. In attending to its people focus, the team discusses how best to serve people by means of appropriate ministries of encouragement, faith development, and comfort. In attending to program/task focus, the team devotes itself to the planning and accomplishment of its vision. What timelines and checklists are needed?

What linkage between the team's ministry and other congregational ministries is appropriate or necessary?

If these elements of team life are spread over a two-hour period, the meeting agenda might look like this:

7:00	**Gather**	Chat
7:10	**Word**	Briefly share a passage of Scripture
7:25	**Share**	Briefly share personal needs and blessings
7:40	**People focus**	Review immediate people issues. Who among those the team serves is new? Hurting or absent? Ready to grow spiritually? Open to joining a small group? Who will follow through with whom? Determine this based on team members' relationships with these individuals or the team members' gifts and overall team responsibility.
8:00	**Prayer**	Pray for the personal needs of ministry-team members. Pray for the people your team serves by name. Pray for the event, activity, or project in which the team is engaging. Prayer is placed here on the agenda rather than at the end of the meeting for two reasons. First, when you move on to program issues, the names and current needs of the people you are serving will already be at the forefront of your minds. Second, if you hold the prayer until after the program discussion, you can easily fail to pray. Program issues, once started, tend to consume the rest of the meeting.
8:15	**Program focus**	Discuss key program/task issues. Work out details after the meeting and between meetings. This is important, because you don't want to consume so much of your time attending to program that you neglect the small-group aspect of the meeting.

9:00 Dismiss   Close with prayer. End on time.

A short (one hour, fifteen minute) ministry-team meeting scheduled during supper or before an evening class, fellowship, or gathering might look like this:

6:00 Gather	Begin eating and chatting
6:10 Word	Briefly share a passage of Scripture
6:25 Share	Briefly share personal needs and blessings
6:40 People focus	Discuss people in the fellowship who are in need of follow-through; determine who will focus on whom.
6:55 Prayer	Pray for ministry-team members and as many people — by name — in your ministry group as possible. If time is short and the list is long, break into groups of four to pray.
7:05 Program focus	Discuss key program issues. Work out details after the meeting.
7:15 Dismiss	End on time

Note: If you're meeting before the large group meeting, go focus on people as the large group gathers.

A schedule for a praise-band team might look more like this:

6:45 Gather	Chat
7:05 Word	Briefly share a passage of Scripture
7:15 Share	Briefly share personal needs and blessings
7:30 People focus	Discuss the music and worship needs of the congregation and ways to better use the ministry of music to inspire worship
7:45 Prayer	Pray for team members and for those you serve by name. Break into groups of four if necessary.

7:55 **Break**

8:00 **Rehearsal**

9:00 **Dismiss**   Close with prayer. End on time

These sample schedules are offered to inspire your thinking about how to find the best way to include the primary team functions of fellowship, people ministry, and program ministry each time your team gathers. (These schedules assume that the details of program decisions are being handled by responsible people between the team meetings.) A team that meets on a weekly basis has more scheduling flexibility. It may choose to devote one meeting a month exclusively to program and planning, or use the two-hour schedule above to have more time to spend on people and program.

Extended meetings may be scheduled for in-depth fellowship-building and highly detailed thinking and praying about next steps. These may be monthly or quarterly events. A very effective way to get together for an extended time is to schedule a retreat during which the team gets away for an evening and the following day. During a retreat, more time can be devoted to each of the three major team concerns as well as dreaming and thinking ahead. There will also be time to just relax and enjoy each other's company.

Bible Verses for Ministry-Team Study

The "Word-Share-Prayer" sequence usually needs to happen in a relatively short period of time in a ministry-team meeting, since a team must accomplish its small group/team fellowship function and its people focus and program focus in one to two hours. For this reason, the Scripture passage studied must necessarily be limited in length. (When the team meets for a longer time, then longer passages may be used.)

You might simply ask the team members to open their Bibles to the text you have chosen, read it and reflect on it silently for five minutes, and then talk about their insights for another ten minutes after that. If you want something a bit more structured, you might try using the Guided Bible Study Sheet, which features a "Read-Reflect-Respond-Request" format. It's an effective way to both guide and limit the Bible study.

As the team begins its meeting, give each member a Guided Bible Study Sheet. Take five to seven minutes to study the text in silence. This will give everyone time to engage what the Bible is saying without distracting conversation. During this time, everyone is invited to read the text, reflect on it, respond to it, and jot down prayer requests they may have. After this period of silence, members can briefly share their insights, make prayer requests, and pray for one another.

The advantage of using these sheets is that writing things down helps people focus on the text, and it gives everyone something to share during the discussion. It also provides a written record of biblical insights and personal concerns that may be kept as both personal and collective journals of the team's spiritual journey.

This kind of Bible-study sheet is easy to prepare. Simply use the basic "Read-Reflect-Respond-Request" format and change the text for each meeting of the team. Because of time contraints, keep the text selections to a few verses. When working up the sheet, you may want to ask general, open-ended questions about the text, as shown in Figure 1.

Figure 1. The Guided Bible Study Sheet with General Questions

READ	[46]And Mary said: "My soul glorifies the Lord [47]and my spirit rejoices in God my Savior, [48]for he has been mindful of the humble state of his servant. From now on all generations will call me blessed, [49]for the Mighty One has done great things for me — holy is his name. . . . [51]He has performed mighty deeds with his arm" (Luke 1:46-49, 51, NIV).
REFLECT	Jot down your insights from the text.
RESPOND	How will you apply the teachings of this text to your own life?
REQUEST	What prayer requests do you have?

Alternatively, you may want to ask specific questions designed to help team members grasp particular insights from the text. Figure 2 uses the same text as that in Figure 1 but features text-specific questions.

Figure 2. The Guided Bible Study Sheet with Specific Questions

READ   ⁴⁶And Mary said: "My soul glorifies the Lord ⁴⁷and my spirit rejoices in God my Savior, ⁴⁸for he has been mindful of the humble state of his servant. From now on all generations will call me blessed, ⁴⁹for the Mighty One has done great things for me — holy is his name. . . . ⁵¹He has performed mighty deeds with his arm" (Luke 1:46-49, 51, NIV).

REFLECT   Mary's song of joy celebrates all that God has done for her.

Jot down some of the "great things" God has done for you in the last year.

RESPOND   Write a brief sentence of praise thanking God for these blessings in your own words, just as Mary sang a song of praise using her own words.

REQUEST   Jot down one area of concern in your life about which you pray that God will do a "great thing."

Whatever translation of the Bible you use, be sure to follow the publisher's rules when it comes to reproduction of their material and copyright acknowledgment. For example, the New International Version of the Bible asks that you put the letters "NIV" after the text as a copyright acknowledgment.

Keep in mind that the Bible texts chosen for a ministry team to study during its "Word-Share-Prayer" sequence are an excellent opportunity to develop and train the team. So it's important to select texts that will enhance team members' faith development, their fellowship with each other, and their ministry.

The following verses and brief passages are geared to equip team members in their ministry-team functions. There are certainly many more texts suitable for ministry-team study; these are only starters to get you going. From your own reading of Scripture, develop a list of those texts that will help your ministry team develop vision and grow in faith and friendship.

Brief Biblical Texts for Ministry-Team Study

Devotion

Exodus 20:8	Sabbath rest
Joshua 1:6-7	courage
Psalm 42:1-2	longing for God
Psalm 130:6	waiting for God
Jeremiah 29:11-14	seeking God wholeheartedly
2 Chronicles 5:11-14	worship
Matthew 6:33	seeking first the kingdom of God
Matthew 7:24-27	obedience
Acts 2:42	devotion to fellowship and prayer
Romans 10:9	confession of faith
Galatians 2:20	living by faith
Ephesians 2:4	mercy
Ephesians 2:8-9	grace
Ephesians 6:18	praying in the Spirit
Philippians 2:5-11	humility
James 1:3	perseverance

James 4:8	resisting Satan
1 Peter 5:5-7	humility
1 Peter 5:8-9	being on the alert
Revelation 3:20	Christ knocking at the door

Quiet Time (Personal Bible Reading and Prayer)

Genesis 12:8, 13:18	Abraham building altars for worship
1 Samuel 30:6	David strengthening himself in God
Daniel 6:13-14	Daniel praying several times a day
Mark 1:35	Jesus going to a solitary place to pray
1 John 1:9	confession

Fellowship

Psalm 133	unity
Matthew 6:14-15	forgiveness
John 13:33-34	loving one another
John 17:20-23	being one
John 18:2	Jesus' small group
Acts 2:42-47	being devoted to fellowship
Acts 14:26-28	sharing what God is doing
Romans 12:3-8	one body with many gifts
Romans 12:18	living in peace with everyone
2 Corinthians 5:18	the ministry of reconciliation
Hebrews 10:25	meeting together

A Heart for Ministry to Others (Having "People Eyes")

Jeremiah 29:7	vision for the city
Ezekiel 22:30	standing in the gap
Luke 19:1-10	Jesus singling out Zacchaeus
Luke 22:32	strengthening the brethren
John 1:35-42	Jesus' first disciples
John 1:43-50	Jesus calling more disciples
John 21:15-17	nurturing others in the faith
Romans 12:4-6	gifts of ministry
Galatians 4:19	laboring to form Christ in others
2 Timothy 2:1-3	passing the faith on to others
1 Peter 4:10	spiritual gifts

Defining Practices of Transformational Ministry

Witness

Matthew 28:19-20	making disciples of all nations
John 1:11-13	Christ's witness
Acts 1:8	being Christ's witnesses
Acts 16:29-32	witness of Paul and Silas
2 Timothy 2:1-3	Paul urging witness
1 Peter 3:15	explaining the hope within
1 John 1:1-3	witnessing to "what we have seen and heard"

Prayer

1 Chronicles 29:10-14	praise and thanksgiving
Nehemiah 1:4-11	confession, supplication
Matthew 6:9-13	The Lord's Prayer
Acts 4:29-30	prayer for God to work wonders
Ephesians 3:16-19	prayer for inner strength
Colossians 1:9-12	prayer to know God's will
Colossians 4:12	prayer for spiritual maturity

Care

1 Samuel 23:16	encouragement
Matthew 25:34-36	compassion
Mark 1:41	compassion
2 Corinthians 1:3-4	comforting those in affliction
Galatians 6:2	bearing one another's burdens
1 Thessalonians 5:11	encouraging one another
James 5:16	confessing to and praying for one another
James 5:13-16	anointing and praying for healing

Word

Psalm 19:9-10	God's word is sweeter than honey
Psalm 119:105	God's word is a light to my path
Isaiah 55:11	God's word will not return empty
Jeremiah 23:29	God's word is like fire
1 Thessalonians 2:13	God's word works in those who believe

2 Timothy 3:16-17   The Word of God is inspired
Hebrews 4:12   The word of God is sharper than any
two-edged sword

"With Me"

Psalm 23:4   God with me
Matthew 1:23   basis of "with me": God with us
Matthew 9:9   "Follow me" = come with me
Mark 3:14   the "with me" principle
Acts 13:1   "prophets and teachers": the ministry team
Acts 20:1-6   Paul and "the magnificent seven":
the ministry team
Romans 16:1-6   network of relationships: "with me"
in friendship
1 Peter 4:9   hospitality: "with me" in my home and life

Send

Isaiah 6:8   "Send me!"
Matthew 9:38   prayer for workers to be sent in mission
Matthew 10:5   Jesus sending the Twelve
Mark 11:1-3   Jesus sending by two's
John 20:21   "I am sending you"
Acts 13:2-4   Barnabas and Paul sent

A Ministry-Team Checklist

A ministry team is any gathering of God's people for the purpose of mutual encouragement in Christ and engagement in the service of Christ. Ministry-team life embraces three movements: discipleship, fellowship, and ministry. The team ministry has a double focus, with members attending to the people they serve in ministry and attending to the tasks their ministry requires. Use this checklist periodically to assess how your team is doing.

A Ministry-Team Checklist

The Beginning Ministry Team

Element One: Clarify the team's vision
Element Two: Identify the new team leader and the leadership core
Element Three: Invite the beginning ministry team together
Element Four: Engage the ministry team in discipleship and fellowship
Element Five: Guide the ministry team in interpersonal ministry and organizing to accomplish its vision

The Ministry Team in Fellowship

Have we established our team's covenantal agreements, and do we review them regularly?

Are we nurturing friendship and discipleship among us?

Are we enjoying small-group life as a team? Do we spend twenty minutes a meeting in "Word-Share-Prayer"?

Are we sharing meals together? Do we have the dates for our quarterly meals in our datebooks?

Have we made prayer partnerships among team members? Are we rotating prayer partners each month?

Have we scheduled an annual overnight retreat?

The Ministry Team in Personal Ministry

Do our team members engage in personal ministry to those we are serving as a team?

Are we praying for them by name?

Do we follow through with people who are new, absent, or going through a difficult time?

Do we focus on individuals using all six of the defining practices of interpersonal ministry? Do we bear witness to them? Do we pray for them? Do we care for them, showing hospitality to them? Do we impart the Word to them, spend time with them, and send them to serve?

Have we engaged those whom we serve in small-group life?

The Ministry Team in Task Ministry

Do we regularly review our ministry, think ahead, and determine our next steps?

Are we assessing the needs of the people we serve before deciding what our tasks and programs are going to be?

Do we have plans linking needs assessment and our defining vision with specific tasks, timelines, and deadlines?

Have we sought to identify and engage each member's spiritual gifts and personal interests and abilities?

Do our team members each have task responsibilities that enable our joint ministry?

Are we developing each member's gifts and leadership skills?

INFORMATION ON
THE VITAL CHURCHES INSTITUTE

E. Stanley Ott is pastor of the Pleasant Hills Community Presbyterian Church and president of the Vital Churches Institute and Vital Faith Resources.

The Vital Churches Institute serves to enable growth in the vitality and effectiveness of the local church. The institute offers seminars on principles and practices of personal spiritual growth and of vital congregational life and leadership, such as "The Acts 16:5 Initiative"®, "Growing a Vital Church"®, and "Developing Leadership for the Vital Church." The institute offers materials on these subjects through Vital Faith Resources.

To learn more about the Vital Churches Institute and Vital Faith Resources, access the following Web sites:

> http://www.VitalChurchesInstitute.com
>   and
> http://www.vitalfaithresources.com.

You may correspond with Stan at

> estanleyott@VitalChurchesInstitute.com.

To receive Stan's free weekly letter of encouragement, go to

> www.buildingoneanother.org.

For information and links on ministry teams, go to

http://www.transformyourchurchwithministryteams.org.

For information on the seminars, or to order additional copies of this book and other materials to help you grow a vital church, you can go to

http://www.VitalChurchesInstitute.com

or write to this address:

The Vital Churches Institute
P.O. Box 18378
Pittsburgh, PA 15236

Ministry Teams

Bandy, Thomas G. *Coaching Change*. Nashville: Abingdon Press, 2000.

————. "Starting the Shift to a Team-Based Organization." *Net Results* 22, no. 2 (February 2001): 3-5.

Barna, George. *The Power of Team Leadership: Achieving Success through Shared Responsibility*. Colorado Springs: WaterBrook Press, 2001.

Bauknight, Brian Kelley. *Body Building: Creating a Ministry Team through Spiritual Gifts*. Nashville: Abingdon Press, 1996.

Blanchard, Ken; Donald Carew; and Eunice Parisi-Carew. *The One-Minute Manager Builds High-Performing Teams*. New York: William Morrow, 2000.

Center for Collaborative Organizations (formerly The Center for the Study of Work Teams): www.workteams.unt.edu.

Cladis, George. *Leading the Team-Based Church: How Pastors and Church Staffs Can Grow Together in a Powerful Fellowship of Leaders*. San Francisco: Jossey-Bass, 1999.

Cordeiro, Wayne. *Doing Church as a Team*. Ventura, Calif.: Regal Books, 2001.

Dotlich, David L., and James L. Noel. *Action Learning: How the World's Top Companies Are Re-Creating Their Leaders and Themselves*. San Francisco: Jossey-Bass, 1998.

Easum, William M. *Leadership on the Other Side*. Nashville: Abingdon Press, 2000.

————. *Sacred Cows Make Gourmet Burgers*. Nashville: Abingdon Press, 1995.

Easum, William M., and Thomas G. Bandy. *Growing Spiritual Redwoods*. Nashville: Abingdon Press, 1997.

Easum, Bandy, and Associates: www.easumbandy.com.

Fisher, Kimball. *Leading Self-Directed Work Teams*. New York: McGraw-Hill, 1999.

Galloway, Dale. *Building Teams in Ministry*. Kansas City: Beacon Hill Press, 2001.

Hestenes, Roberta. *Turning Committees into Communities*. Colorado Springs: NavPress, 1991.

Hook, M. Anne Burnette, and Shirley F. Clement. *Staying Focused: Building Ministry Teams for Christian Formation*. Nashville: Discipleship Resources, 2002.

Iverson, Dick, with Ray Grant. *Team Ministry: Putting Together a Team That Makes Churches Grow*. Portland, Ore.: City Bible Publishing, 1989.

Jennings, Ken, and John Stahl-Wert. *The Serving Leader*. San Francisco: Berrett-Koehler Publishers, Inc., 2003.

Katzenbach, Jon R., and Douglas K. Smith. *The Wisdom of Teams: Creating the High-Performance Organization*. New York: HarperCollins, 1994.

————. *The Discipline of Teams: A Mindbook-Workbook for Delivering Small Group Performance*. New York: John Wiley & Sons, 2001.

Leadership Network: www.leadnet.org.

Lencioni, Patrick M. *The Five Dysfunctions of a Team: A Leadership Fable*. San Francisco: Jossey-Bass, 2002.

Maxwell, John C. *The Seventeen Essential Qualities of a Team Player: Becoming the Kind of Person Every Team Wants*. Nashville: Thomas Nelson, 2002.

————. *The Seventeen Indisputable Laws of Teamwork: Embrace Them and Empower Your Team*. Nashville: Thomas Nelson, 2001.

McIntosh, Gary L. *Staff Your Church for Growth: Building Team Ministry in the Twenty-First Century*. Grand Rapids: Baker Book House, 2000.

Net Results Magazine: New Ideas for Vital Ministries: www.netresults.org.

Olsen, Charles M. *Transforming Church Boards into Communities of Spiritual Leaders*. Herndon. Va.: The Alban Institute, 1995.

Pell, Arthur R. *The Complete Idiot's Guide to Team Building.* Tucson: Alpha Books, 1999.

Reeves, R. Daniel. "Practical Advice for Launching Teams." *Ministry Advantage* 8, no. 1 (Winter 1998). See www.fuller.edu/c11/ma/ma8.1/html/reeves4.html.

————. "Mega-Shifting to Team Ministry." *Ministry Advantage* 8, no. 1. For this article and several other excellent articles on team-based ministry, see www.fuller.edu/cll/ma/ma8.1 or www.homestead-.com/nppn/files/Article008.htm.

Senge, Peter M. *The Fifth Discipline.* New York: Doubleday, 1990.

Shey, Stephen L., and Walt Kallestad. *Team Ministry.* Nashville: Abingdon Press, 1996.

Slaughter, Michael. *The Power of Teams: Ginghamsburg on Worship.* Available at www.ginghamsburg.org/bookstor/power.htm.

Sweet, Leonard I. *AquaChurch: Essential Leadership Arts for Piloting Your Church in Today's Fluid Culture.* Loveland, Colo.: Group Publishing, 1999.

Vital Churches Institute: www.VitalChurchesInstitute.com.

Warner, Greg. *The Power of Teams.* Available at www.faithworks.com/archives/power_teams.htm.

Defining Vision and Defining Practices

Bandy, Thomas. *Moving Off the Map.* Nashville: Abingdon Press, 1998.

Barna, George. *The Power of Vision: How You Can Capture and Apply God's Vision for Your Ministry.* Ventura, Calif.: Regal Books, 1997.

————. *Turning Vision into Action.* Ventura: Regal Books, 1997.

Callahan, Kennon. *Twelve Keys to an Effective Church.* San Francisco: HarperSanFrancisco, 1983.

Collins, James C., and Jerry I. Porras. *Built to Last: Successful Habits of Visionary Companies.* New York: HarperCollins, 1994.

Easum, William, and Thomas Bandy. *Growing Spiritual Redwoods.* Nashville: Abingdon Press, 1997.

Logan, Robert E. *Beyond Church Growth: Action Plans for Developing a Dynamic Church.* Old Tappan, N.J.: Fleming H. Revell, 1989.

Malphurs, Aubrey. *Values-Driven Leadership: Discovering and Developing*

Your Core Values for Ministry. Grand Rapids: Baker Book House, 1994.

McClaren, Brian. *The Church on the Other Side*. Grand Rapids: Zondervan, 2000.

McIntosh, Gary L. *One Size Doesn't Fit All*. Old Tappan, N.J.: Fleming H. Revell, 1999.

McManus, Erwin. *An Unstoppable Force: Daring to Become the Church God Had in Mind*. Loveland, Colo.: Group Publishing, 2001.

Missional Leadership Institute: www.mliweb.net. See especially "Engaging the Missional Realities of Western Cultures."

Nanus, Burt. *Visionary Leadership: Creating a Compelling Sense of Direction for Your Organization*. San Francisco: Jossey-Bass, 1995.

Ott, E. Stanley. *Twelve Dynamic Shifts for Transforming Your Church*. Grand Rapids: Eerdmans, 2002.

————. *The Vibrant Church*. Ventura, Calif.: Regal Books, 1989. Available from www.vitalfaithresources.com.

————. *Vision for a Vital Church*. Pittsburgh: Vital Faith Resources, 1994. Available at www.vitalfaithresources.com.

Riddell, Mark; Mark Pierson; and Cathy Kirkpatrick. *The Prodigal Project: Journey into the Emerging Church*. London: SPCK, 2000.

Schuller, Robert H. *Your Church Has Real Possibilities*. Ventura, Calif.: Regal Books, 1974.

Schwartz, Christiansen A. *Natural Church Development: A Guide to Eight Essential Qualities of Healthy Churches*. Carol Stream, Ill.: Church-Smart Resources, 1996.

Smith, Chuck, Jr. *The End of the World as We Know It*. Colorado Springs: WaterBrook Press, 2001.

Sweet, Leonard. *Aquachurch: Essential Leadership Arts for Piloting Your Church in Today's Fluid Culture*. Loveland, Colo.: Group Publishing, 1999.

Warren, Rick. *The Purpose Driven Church*. Grand Rapids: Zondervan, 1995.

Fostering of Discipleship

ALPHA (contemporary evangelism and discipleship): www.alphacourse .org.

Arn, Win, and Charles Arn. *The Master's Plan for Making Disciples: Every Christian an Effective Witness through an Enabling Church*. Grand Rapids: Baker Book House, 1998.

Barna, George. *Growing True Disciples: New Strategies for Producing Genuine Followers of Christ*. Colorado Springs: WaterBrook Press, 2001.

Church Discipleship Ministry by the Navigators: http://home.navigators.org/us/cdm/index.cfm.

Coleman, Robert E. *The Master Plan of Discipleship*. Grand Rapids: Baker Book House, 1998.

————. *The Master Plan of Evangelism*. Old Tappan, N.J.: Fleming H. Revell, 1993.

Disciple Bible Study Program: www.cokesbury.com.

Foster, Richard. *Celebration of Discipline*. San Francisco: Harper & Row, 1988.

Hull, Bill. *The Disciple-Making Church*. Old Tappan, N.J.: Fleming H. Revell, 1998.

————. *The Disciple-Making Pastor*. Grand Rapids: Baker Book House, 1999.

Hybels, Bill, and Mark Mittelberg. *Becoming a Contagious Christian*. Grand Rapids: Zondervan, 1996.

Johnson, Ben Campbell. *Living before God*. Grand Rapids: Eerdmans, 2000.

Linn, Jan G. *Reclaiming Evangelism: A Practical Guide for Mainline Churches*. St. Louis: Chalice, 1998.

McDonald, Glenn W. *The Disciplemaking Church: From Dry Bones to Spiritual Vitality*. Grand Haven, Mich.: FaithWalk Publishing, 2004.

McLaren, Brian D. *A New Kind of Christian*. San Francisco: Jossey-Bass, 2001.

Ogden, Greg. *Discipleship Essentials: A Guide to Building Your Life in Christ*. Downers Grove, Ill.: InterVarsity Press, 1998.

Omega Discipleship Ministries: www.omega-discipleship.com. See especially the "Resources for Discipleship."

Ortberg, John. *The Life You've Always Wanted*. Grand Rapids: Zondervan, 2002.

Ott, E. Stanley. *The Joy of Discipling*. Grand Rapids: Zondervan, 1989. Available from www.vitalfaithresources.com.

REV Magazine: www.rev-magazine.com.

Willard, Dallas. *The Divine Conspiracy*. New York: HarperCollins, 1999.

————. *The Spirit of the Disciplines*. San Francisco: HarperCollins, 1991.

Small-Group Life

Arnold, Jeffrey. *The Big Book on Small Groups*. Downers Grove, Ill.: InterVarsity Press, 1992.

————. *Small Group Outreach: Turning Groups Inside Out*. Downers Grove, Ill.: InterVarsity Press, 1998.

Borthwick, Paul, et al. *Small Group Ministry*. Loveland, Colo.: Vital Ministry Books, 1999.

Donahue, Bill. *Leading Life-Changing Small Groups*. Grand Rapids: Zondervan, 1996.

Donahue, Bill, and Russ Robinson. *Building a Church of Small Groups*. Grand Rapids: Zondervan, 2001.

George, Carl F. *Prepare Your Church for the Future*. Old Tappan, N.J.: Fleming H. Revell, 1991.

George, Carl F., with Warren Bird. *Nine Keys to Effective Small Group Leadership*. Mansfield, Ohio: Kingdom Publishing, 1997.

Icenogle, Gareth Weldon. *Biblical Foundations for Small Group Ministry: An Integrational Approach*. Downers Grove, Ill.: InterVarsity Press, 1994.

Meyer, Richard C. *One Anothering, Volume 1: Biblical Building Blocks for Small Groups*. Philadelphia: Innisfree Press, 1990.

————. *One Anothering, Volume 2: Building Spiritual Community in Small Groups*. Philadelphia: Innisfree Press, 1999.

————. *One Anothering, Volume 3: Creating Significant Spiritual Community*. Philadelphia: Innisfree Press, 2003.

Ott, E. Stanley. *Small Group Life*. Available from www.vitalfaithresources.com.

Small Group Network: www.smallgroups.com. This site has extensive small-group resources.

Ministry Mobilization

Bauknight, Brian Kelley. *Body Building: Creating a Ministry Team through Spiritual Gifts.* Nashville: Abingdon Press, 1996.

Bugbee, Bruce L.; Don Cousins; and Bill Hybels. *Network: Understanding God's Design for You in the Church.* Grand Rapids: Zondervan, 1994.

Church Growth Institute: www.churchgrowth.org.

Connextion: www.connextion.org. See especially "Equipping People for Ministry and Maturity."

Cordeiro, Wayne. *Doing Church as a Team.* Ventura, Calif.: Regal Books, 2001. See also the DESIGN approach of Wayne Cordeiro and the New Hope Christian Fellowship at www.eNewHope.org.

Gilbert, Larry. *Team Ministry: How to Find Meaning and Fulfillment through Understanding the Spiritual Gifts within You.* Oxnard, Calif.: Church Growth Institute, 1992.

Kise, Jane A. G.; David Stark; and Sandra Krebs Hirsh. *Lifekeys: Discovering Who You Are, Why You're Here, What You Do Best.* Bloomington: Bethany House, 1996.

LifeKeys: www.LifeKeys.com.

Mallory, Sue. *The Equipping Church.* Grand Rapids: Zondervan, 2001.

Mallory, Sue, and Brad Smith. *Equipping Church Guidebook.* Grand Rapids: Zondervan, 2001.

Ogden, Greg. *The New Reformation: Returning the Ministry to the People of God.* Grand Rapids: Zondervan, 1990.

SHAPE ministry of Saddleback Church: www.saddleback.com.

Warren, Rick. *The Purpose Driven Church.* Grand Rapids: Zondervan, 1995.

Action Learning, Thinking Ahead, and Change

Biehl, Bob. *Masterplanning: A Complete Guide for Building a Strategic Plan for Your Business, Church, or Organization.* Nashville: Broadman & Holman Publishers, 1997.

Garvin, David A. *Learning in Action: A Guide to Putting the Learning Organization to Work.* Boston: Harvard Business School Press, 2003.

Herrington, Jim; Mike Bonem; and James H. Furr. *Leading Congregational Change.* San Francisco: Jossey-Bass, 2000.

Johnson, Spencer. *Who Moved My Cheese?* New York: G. P. Putnam's Sons, 1998.

Kotter, John P. *Leading Change.* Boston: Harvard Business School Press, 1996.

Malphurs, Aubrey. *Advanced Strategic Planning: A New Model for Church and Ministry Leaders.* Grand Rapids: Baker Book House, 1999.

Marquardt, Michael J. *Action Learning in Action: Transforming Problems and People for World-Class Organizational Learning.* Palo Alto, Calif.: Davies-Black Publishing, 1999.

————. *Optimizing the Power of Action Learning: Solving Problems and Building Leaders in Real Time.* Palo Alto, Calif.: Davies-Black Publishing, 2004.

McGill, Ian, and Liz Beaty. *Action Learning: A Guide for Professional, Management, and Educational Development.* London: Kogan Page Ltd., 2001.

Rothwell, William J. *The Action Learning Guidebook: A Real-Time Strategy for Problem Solving, Training Design, and Employee Development.* San Francisco: Jossey-Bass/Pfeiffer, 1999.

Shelley, Marshall. *Renewing Your Church through Vision and Planning: Thirty Strategies to Transform Your Ministry,* vol. 2 of the Library of Leadership Development. Minneapolis: Bethany House, 1997.

Weinstein, Krystyna. *Action Learning: A Practical Guide for Managers.* Aldershot, Hampshire, U.K.: Gower Publishing Co., 1998.